Thinking about
God and Morality

Lesley Parry

Hodder Murray
A MEMBER OF THE HODDER HEADLINE GROUP

Acknowledgements

Thanks to Swifty and Janet D. for proofreading and offering sage words of advice in the production of this book. Thanks to Holly and Sarah for being guinea pigs on chunks of the book, and to my Y10 classes for testing isolated bits. Thanks to JRH for the suggestions, examples, ideas and general all-round support and encouragement whilst writing it.

AKG Photo pages 21, 30 (left), 64 (top right), 95; Associated Press/JAB page 35 (right), AP/Misha Japaridze page 34 (bottom), AP/Bebeto Matthews page 35 (left), AP/Murad Sezer page 73 (middle left), AP/Nick Ut page 83 (bottom left), AP/Obed Zilwa page 64 (bottom), AP page 64 (left), AP page 73 (top & middle right), AP page 83 (bottom right), AP page 88 (bottom); Bruce Coleman Collection/Jeff Foott page 9 (bottom), Felix Labhardt page 31 (bottom), Robert Maier page 98 (middle and left), Hans Reinhard pages 9 (top right), 98 (top), Colin Varndell page 9 (top left); CEWC and Tibet Support Group UK page 88 (top); Circa Photo Library/John Smith page 50 (right); Corbis pages 6, 15, 93; Corbis/Craig Aurness page 4; Corbis/Burstein Collection page 23; Corbis/Phil Emmett page 23 (bottom); Corbis/Marc Garanger page 5 (right); Corbis/Philip Gould page 32; Corbis/Arne Hodalic page 33 (bottom); Corbis/Christine Osborne page 23 (middle); Corbis/Reflections Photolibrary page 38 (2nd from top); Corbis/Galen Rowell page 34 (top); Corbis/S.I.N page 38 (middle); Corbis/David &

Peter Turnley pages 33 (middle), 38 (bottom); Corbis/Bill Varie page 46 (bottom); Corbis/Wild Country page 5 (left); Format Photographers/Jacky Chapman page 45 (right), Format Photographers/Ulrike Preuss page 51 (bottom right); Kate Harrison page 7; Life File/ Mike Evans page 67 (middle), Jeremy Hoare page 63 (bottom left), Emma Lee pages 47 (top), 62 (bottom left), 99 (right), Mike Maidment page 67 (bottom right), Angela Maynard page 67 (bottom left), Louise Oldroyd page 33 (top), Richard Powers pages 62 (middle right), 67 (top left), Jan Suttle page 45 (left), Nicola Sutton page 63 (bottom right), Flora Torrance page 62 (middle left), 99 (left), Andrew Ward pages 38 (bottom right), 63 (top right), 67 (middle right); Methodist Church website page 96, PA Photos/Arnold James Arnold page 69 (bottom), PA Photos/Michael Crabtree page 68, PA Photos/European Press Agency page 69 (top), 83 (top left), 97 (right), PA Photos/David Giles page 71 (bottom); Caroline Penn page 73 (bottom); RSPCA/Mark Votier page 91 (top left), pages 91 (middle right, bottom left), 96, 97 (left), 98 (bottom right); Peter Sanders page 30; Science Photo Library pages 2, Science Photo Library/Mehau Kulyk page 31 (top), 42; Still Pictures/Jacques Jangoux page 91(bottom right), Still Pictures/I.Lloyd page 91 (middle left); Telegraph Colour Library pages 3, 46 (middle), 47 (bottom); Werner Forman Archive, Philip Goldman Collection, London page 89 (top right).

AQA (NEAB) AQA examination questions are reproduced by permission of the Assessment and Qualifications Alliance.

Orders: please contact Bookpoint Ltd, 130 Milton Park, Abingdon, Oxon OX14 4SB. Telephone: (44) 01235 827720, Fax: (44) 01235 400454. Lines are open from 9.00 – 6.00, Monday to Saturday, with a 24 hour message answering service. You can order through our website www.hodderheadline.co.uk

British Library Cataloguing in Publication Data
A catalogue record for this title is available from The British Library

ISBN 0 340 79966 8

First published 2002

Impression number   10 9 8 7 6 5

Year   2007 2006 2005

Copyright © 2002 Lesley Parry

Cover photo from Photodisc.

Typeset by Liz Rowe.

Printed in Italy for Hodder Murray, an imprint of Hodder Education, a member of the Hodder Headline group, 338 Euston Road, London NW1 3BH

Contents

► Introduction

This book has been written specifically to meet the AQA Specification B Module 1 syllabus. It follows the outline, moving through the topics in the order given by the syllabus. It is informed additionally by the syllabus being replaced by Specification B Module I, and many of the sample questions come from papers for that syllabus (AQA Syllabus D).

It can be read in two halves – firstly, the *Thinking about God* half, which is essentially philosophical; secondly, *Thinking about Morality*, which is morality-based. These are met within the new Specification in the two halves of the exam paper. *Philosophy* is to be examined via one compulsory stimulus-based question divided into short-answer parts, and one compulsory structured essay. *Morality* will be examined via a choice of two structured essays from a selection of four offered. You can see an example of how the paper should look at the back of this book.

The Units within cover the topics from a variety of angles as well as providing the necessary information required by those studying for the exam. Each Unit asks students to think about what they are being told and about the implications of the issues. Knowledge and understanding of the topics are important, but ability to apply that knowledge is vital to the highest grades for this Specification. The style of the text is designed to encourage and develop exactly that.

The Specification requires that students respond in the second part of the paper from two religious traditions. The phrase *religious tradition* is used to encompass centres who wish to study two Christian traditions (denominations) and those who wish to twin their Christian study with a non-Christian major world faith. The structure of Units 6 to 10 allows both. For each topic, two Christian denominations are considered, followed by two non-Christian major world faiths. It should be remembered that the exam requires at least one Christian tradition – 'Exemplification and illustration of answers to examination questions are required to be provided from the perspective either of Christianity and another world religion, or of two denominations within Christianity' *(AQA GCSE Religious Studies Specification B, p 12, 2003 Spec)*. Any answer within the exam giving two faiths other than Christianity can then only possibly gain half the available marks. Students are not required to use the same traditions for every answer, hence the range of traditions met in this textbook. Indeed, for some topics it is easier to pick on a religious tradition never otherwise used.

At the end of each Unit is an *Exam Tips* section. This is written to give some insight into the style of questions and the way to answer them. It also tries to give useful tips about addressing questions – common mistakes, trigger words etc. Each *Exam Tips* is different, so that together they provide a good grounding to give confidence to students. Good exam technique improves grades and it is hoped that this element will improve exam technique.

Within each Unit, there are cross-references to point students to linked ideas elsewhere in the book. They provide additional ideas and points within answers which often take the candidate's work into the higher levels. The better candidates will see and use such links in their responses.

At the end of the book are three important sections. Firstly, there is a Revision Outline section, which gives a basic guide to each topic – what students need to know. Secondly, there is a Sample Paper to give students an example of what they might face. The idea is to familiarise them and to engender confidence. Thirdly, a Glossary provides all the major words which students need to know. These words are often defined in the body of the work, especially in the case of the morality Units, but in the Glossary they are gathered together.

1 The Existence of God

With a partner, make a list of reasons why people say God does exist, and why they say God doesn't exist.

Read the quotations below. People who believe in God's existence are **theists**. Which ones are theists?

People who don't believe in God's existence are **atheists**. Which ones are atheists?

People who are unsure of God's existence, or believe it can't be proved either way, are known as **agnostics**.

> The Guru Granth Sahib tells me all I need to know about God. It is God's message to each of us.

> God? I'll believe in God when I see him!

> My gran died and she always helped people. God didn't save her, even though she was a good person. In fact, she suffered too much. Where is God, eh?

> Look at nature — it is so cruel. Animals kill each other, natural disasters everywhere — it's pure luck anything survives.

> If there is no God, how did everything else come to exist? Something must have started it.

> God spoke to me in a dream. I felt really comforted by God's presence — it gave me hope.

> We don't need God. Science can supply us with all the answers — Big Bang, evolution . . . God is just like the joker in the pack — a cover until we get the real reason.

> The earth and the heavens are very complicated. Look at the beauty of the earth in orbit. It follows its path without error. Look at how the earth rotates in such a manner that we do not notice its rotation. Look at water: a simple substance, yet it is made up of billions of atoms. If you see footprints, you conclude that a human has been there, so if you look at the heavens — their beauty and complexity — how can you but conclude that God is there — an all-wise Creator?

These are reasons why people believe in God or don't believe. The origins of life, seeming design in nature, meeting God, all lead people to believe in God. Science and its answers, chaotic nature, and never having met God are common causes of disbelief. We will look at these types of arguments for or against God's existence in this course.

How It All Began – Origins of the Universe

The Big Bang Theory

This theory claims that time began with a huge explosion about 20 billion years ago. The explosion came from nothing (matter and antimatter combining). From the explosion a huge cloud of dust and gases was formed, which eventually became the universe – our sun, the planets, and earth. Life developed on earth after this. Human life is as recent as five million years old.

What evidence is there of this? An explosion causes everything to be flung outwards. Since there is no gravity in space, an object that is caused to move keeps on moving forever (unless another force acts upon it). Astronomers say the universe is still expanding – as if that explosion is still being felt. There is also the trace of an explosion in the form of background microwave radiation. Explosions cause radiation and this can still be observed in space.

So How Did Life Begin?

According to this theory, the earliest signs of life appeared millions of years ago, before the land and sea were even formed. The land and sea had not settled, and the temperature on earth was much greater than it is today. This is called the primeval soup. Within this were the proteins and amino acids required for life. Somehow these were fused together and life was created. The first life forms, after these single-cellular beings, were insects. From these came the fish and birds, then reptiles and mammals, then humans.

It is unlikely that you will be asked for a detailed description of a scientific theory. You may well be expected to refer to it and explain yourself briefly. For example, in answering a question about why some people don't believe the world was created by God, you might explain that they believe in the Big Bang Theory, which says the universe came from a huge explosion, so it had nothing to do with God. Alternatively, you might be asked if it is possible to believe in both science and God. You could answer that some people believe God caused the Big Bang to happen, so obviously it is. So you do need to have at least an idea about these theories.

The Basics

①

Use your own words to explain the Big Bang Theory.

②

Does God figure in this scientific theory? Is it possible to believe in this theory and in the existence of God? How?

③

This is a *theory*. What does that mean? Is a *theory* the same as a *proof*? Does it matter?

▶ God as First Cause

Think about the world around you and all the things in it. Can you think of anything which is not caused by something else? Anything that is totally independent?

Maybe you can't. It seems that everything relies on something else for its occurrence, its existence, its being. For example, a row of dominoes doesn't just fall over – it must have some force act upon it before the whole chain of dominoes falls in sequence. Usually someone pushes the first one.

We have a problem. We exist, and so does the world around us. We don't know of anything that can cause itself though, so how can anything exist now? It isn't logical.

If things happen because of other things causing them to happen, and if we want to believe there was a beginning to the universe, we have to have something to start it all off. What was it?

There has to have been an Uncaused Cause, a **First Cause** that did not rely on anything else. Some people would call God that First Cause.

You might say: 'Of course, it's the Big Bang! The Big Bang is the First Cause.' Funny though that we don't say: 'Ah yes, but what caused the Big Bang?' Think about it!

The Basics

① In your own words explain the idea of God as First Cause.

② Is it possible to believe in God as First Cause and a scientific theory about the origins of the universe? How?

Person Profile

St Thomas Aquinas was a Christian monk, who lived from 1225–1274 CE. He wrote several books, including *Summa Theologica*, which gave his *proofs* of God's existence. He spoke of five different proofs. The second is about God being the Uncaused Cause, the First Cause of everything else. So, according to Aquinas – using the process of argument on this page – God was the cause of the universe.

► The Creation of the Universe

For the exam you need to be able to write out one **creation** story from a religious tradition. There are two in this unit, but the one from **Genesis** is common to several religious traditions – Christianity, Judaism and Islam.

The Genesis Creation Story

See if you can jot down the elements of the Genesis creation story, before you read a description of it. You can find it in Genesis chapter 1 to chapter 2 verse 3.

Genesis is the first book in the **Bible** (Christianity), and the first book of the five, which make up the **Torah** (Judaism). Islam accepts its truth.

In Genesis we are told that God created the world in seven days, including a day of rest. Before the creation there was nothing. We are told that on each of the six actual creation days, God created something extra until the world was complete. On day one, light; day two, the heavens (firmament); day three, land and water, and vegetation; day four, the sun, moon and stars; day five, fish and birds; day six, animals and man. At the end of each day's creating, God looked at what He had done, and claimed that it was good.

Genesis as a Myth

If I believe this interpretation of creation stories, then I don't believe God told them directly to mankind. I believe whoever wrote them was inspired by the world around them and a sense of God. This means that I shouldn't try to read them as versions of what happened. Instead they are answering questions like 'Why did the world come to be?' and 'Have I got a purpose on earth?' In the case of creation stories, the writer is trying to show that we each have a place in the world, and that the world is a good place. So it doesn't matter whether science can prove the story wrong, because the story isn't trying to state facts anyway.

► *What interpretation of one of the creation stories would this view give? Does it seem reasonable to you? Explain yourself.*

The Basics

①
Write in your own words one creation story from these pages. You could do this as a cartoon.

②
Creation stories can be understood in a variety of ways. Explain each way.

③
Can a person believe in a scientific view of the origins of the universe and still believe in Genesis?
Explain how.

Understanding Creation Stories

There are three ways to interpret holy scriptures and their creation stories; as a myth, in a fundamentalist way and in a progressive way.

The Fundamentalist View

If I interpret a creation story in this way, I believe it is literally true. Every word in it is the word of God, who is always correct, and tells only the truth. God dictated the holy book, including the creation story. Whatever I read in the story must be absolutely correct. It isn't difficult to believe this, as I also believe that God is all-powerful (**omnipotent**) and all-knowing (**omniscient**), so God is more than capable of creating the world.

▶ *What interpretation of one of the creation stories would this view give? Does it seem reasonable to you? Explain yourself.*

The Progressive View

If I interpret a creation story in this way, I believe it is more or less the truth. The holy book, and so the creation story, do tell us what really happened. However, God did not dictate the story, God inspired it. This means that there is room for error in the way it is told. One way to look at the creation stories is to see them as general descriptions. For example, in Genesis, we are told it took seven *days*. The word for day in the original language can mean *period of time*, so maybe that's actually what it meant. Maybe it is saying that God raised the level of the development of the world at regular intervals over a long period of time, the most crucial example being when God created humans.

▶ *What interpretation of one of the creation stories would this view give? Does it seem reasonable to you? Explain yourself.*

A Hindu Creation Story

In Hindu belief, God creates the world. God sustains it and is also responsible for its destruction. Hindus believe that the world is being created and destroyed, created and destroyed in a never-ending cycle. These three major roles of God are represented by the **Trimurti** – the three major forms of God in Hinduism (Brahma, Vishnu and Shiva).

Followers of Vishnu (Vaishnavas) believe that Vishnu is the real form of God. They claim that before it is time for the new cycle of creation, Vishnu sleeps on a cobra. Then he wakes up, and Brahma grows from his navel. Once grown, Brahma creates the world. Vishnu then takes on the role of preserving the world by protecting it. Vishnu must sometimes come to earth to do that, for example in the form of an **avatar** such as Krisna. When it is time for the cycle of creation to end, Shiva comes from Vishnu's brow. Shiva then destroys the world and Vishnu goes back to sleep until it is time to create again.

► **Nature – Such Design!**

Read the following. After each bit of information, you are asked to think, and make some observations, before you read on.

Imagine you are walking in the middle of nowhere – perhaps on a hike through the countryside. You trip over something stuck in the ground. Cursing it, you see that it is a mechanical object, which you have never seen the like of before. You pick it up to look at it. You can see the object in this picture. *What questions might you have about it?*

Someone tells you that the object is natural, not man-made. *Do you believe them? What evidence can you give to show that it isn't natural?*

So, we can agree that the object is unlikely to be a natural thing. Someone must have made it. We can see that it has a purpose – it is for doing something, even if we don't know what that something is. It has a shape, which we don't link to nature.

Then someone tells you that they know experts who will swear that it is natural. You don't know anything about nature or what it can really do, so you should believe them, and stop being so stupid.

► *How do you respond to being challenged by experts, and being told you are too stupid to know anything anyway? What else can you say to defend your belief that the object in the picture is man-made, not natural? Or would you change your mind?!*

So, it's man-made. That's that!

Let's just think about the world around us. In science lessons, you must have learned about cycles within nature. Do you know how the food chain works? Have you ever wondered about the way that day always follows night (or vice versa)? Or how we have seasons that stay in the same order? Think of the animals that are perfectly suited to their environment. Each human is unique. What would the world be like if it was just a degree hotter or colder? And what about the Big Bang? – if that hadn't had the right power and temperature, there'd be no life now!

Some people would look at your list and decide that there were too many things that look deliberate, or look as if they had been thought about. The world looks designed.

But, if it looks designed, then someone (or something) must have designed it: a being of immense intelligence and immense power – unlike anyone in our experience. God maybe?

task

① Think of all the things mentioned above. Make a list of all this evidence of design.

② Split your list into examples showing design in the natural world, and design in humans.

Person Profile

The most famous person to use the **teleological argument** (argument from design) to prove God's existence was William Paley. He was an 18th-century archdeacon in Carlisle. He wrote many books, including *Natural Theology*. His argument followed the process you have just gone through.

Paley used the idea of a watch which looked as if it had been deliberately made as compared to a stone, which was natural. He then decided that the world itself possessed even greater evidence of design because of its interdependent systems. Consequently, just as the watch needed a designer, so did the world. And for Paley the designer was obviously God.

Each one is unique – no two are the same

The food chain

Suited to its environment

Scientifically Speaking

'Did you hear the one about the scientist who believed in God?'

There is a theory called the **Anthropic Principle**, which takes all the evidence you've just used, and a lot more. It comes to the conclusion that there is so much evidence of design that there must have been a designer – a bit like the argument of **William Paley**, but much more high-powered.

Here's how it goes. If anything about our world, or even our universe, had been even slightly different, the world and life as we know it would never have existed. Change gravity by a fraction, change the power of the original explosion, change the elements created in the explosion, change our distance from the sun – any of these would mean life would not exist. It's all so precise, it's as if someone had done it deliberately. Scientists believing this, believe God designed and created the world through the scientific systems we know. This is the **Strong Anthropic Principle**.

task

Think about what you have done in this lesson. You have used the example of an obviously man-made object to go on to suggest that the world, too, may be designed (analogy). Write up your process. Use the following headings to help you: what we observed about our found object; what we decided about its origins; what we observed about the world; what we observed about humans; what we decided about their origin.

►► Check out the notes on General and Special Revelation regarding how God can be known through nature p31, Unit 4.

► Against Design?

Why might some people think the world isn't designed? What evidence is there?

Siamese twins – one must die for either to survive.

Earthquake kills thousands

Floods hit Bangladesh – again tens of thousands are homeless.

It's official – the world is getting hotter

More vCJD deaths – still no sign of a cure

Pure evil – no other explanation for behaviour of killer.

We can challenge the idea that the world is designed because of all the things that happen or that exist, which seem to suggest there is nothing deliberate about the world. The headlines above give some examples and may show some really unfair aspects of nature. Why should Bangladesh always flood and its people suffer? If someone had designed the world, that flaw looks cruel, not just a case of bad design.

Evolution

Look around you at the world and everything in it. Do things change? Do people change? Is there anything that doesn't change?

When you came to high school, it was a big change from life at primary school. If you have moved from one high school to another, that's a big change too. How did you cope with the difference? Do different people cope in different ways?

If you went to live in a very cold country, things would be very different for you. You would have to make changes to your life. What would happen if you didn't?

You have just thought of the main elements of evolutionary theory. When we look at the world around us, we can see many, many different varieties of animals, birds, fish, insects and people. For example, birds with different types of beaks.

If we look at the environment in which these live, we can see there are great differences. For example, some places are much hotter than others. Environments are always changing; volcanoes may erupt covering the surrounding area with ash, altering the shape of the landscape.

We can also see that the creatures in an area are suited to that particular environment. A polar bear has special fur, which makes it possible for it to live in cold temperatures.

Many scientists believe that the world has always been changing. Creatures have had to get used to the change and adapt to it, or they have died. Where a whole species could not adapt, it has become extinct. Where a species did adapt, its biology has changed so that the species survived.

This theory suggests that nothing was designed to look like it does today, or to work in the way it does today. Things have changed so that they would survive, so the idea of design is wrong.

► Weak Anthropic Principle

You've already met this idea if you have covered the topic of work on design (page 7). Here's how it goes: if anything about our world, or even our universe, had been even slightly different, the world and life as we know it would never have existed. Change gravity by a fraction, change the power of the original explosion, change the elements created in the explosion, change our distance from the sun – any of these would mean life never came to exist. However life does exist, so how do we explain that coincidence?

▲ Darwin realised that different places caused different species of the same creature.

▲ The polar bear's coat lets it survive where most animals couldn't.

In this interpretation of that evidence, scientists say that the universe is simply the way it is because it *is* the way it is! We can only ask the question of why we are here because we *are* here. It was all just an amazing fluke, which we can be thankful for, but which we shouldn't read anything into. This interpretation is called the **Weak Anthropic Principle**.

Another way scientists have looked at this is to say that because the universe is so huge, with so many possibilities, there must be life *somewhere*. We are that lucky somewhere. That's what it all is really – luck.

Person Profile

Charles Darwin was a natural scientist. He wrote a book called *Origin of the Species*, published in 1859. This was the culmination of years of research including travels on the scientific exploration ship, HMS Beagle. In *Origin*, Darwin suggested that the world is a place of change, and that the huge variety of creatures and species is the result of thousands of years of change and adaptation. He said that there is a struggle for survival between species. Where species failed to adapt, they became extinct, so that only the fittest (best-suited) could survive. He called this *Natural Selection*.

However, Darwin still claimed God was involved in all this. In the final chapter of *Origin*, Darwin asks where all the intelligence within nature, and the complexity and interdependence came from. He finds it difficult to believe that without some sort of guidance, there isn't just total chaos. He puts it down to God – God created the original lifeforms with the ability to adapt and change. It isn't design down to the fine detail, it is design via intelligence and adaptability.

The Basics

① Some people claim that the world does not look designed. What evidence could someone with that point of view give?

② Explain the idea of evolution. How might it take God out of the picture?

③ How does the Weak Anthropic Principle explain design in the world without God?

④ Is it possible to believe in God *and* evolution? Explain yourself.

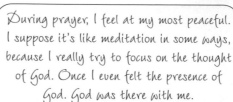

> I believe I have met God through a miracle. God healed my husband after the doctors said he could not be cured. I felt God at work.

► Meeting God

Many people claim to have met God personally. For many who claim not to believe in God, it is the only way they say they'd believe. In other words, it is the strongest form of proof for them.

Meeting God is called a **religious experience** – that is, direct or indirect contact with God. Unit 4 (General and Special Revelation) looks at this in detail.

► *Make a note of all the ways that someone might believe the have felt God's presence or met God. Are some ways better than others? Explain why.*

> During prayer, I feel at my most peaceful. I suppose it's like meditation in some ways, because I really try to focus on the thought of God. Once I even felt the presence of God. God was there with me.

► *Imagine your best friend told you that last night they met God, or felt God's presence. Would you believe them? Why/why not? Make a list of reasons for and against what they say being true.*

Reality or Illusion

Reality is when something is actual; it is that which exists. **Illusion** is a false or misleading perception.

Some people say religious experiences are real. Some say they are an illusion. Some say they can be either.

When someone says they don't believe in God, and certainly not in religious experience, they often point to there being no actual proof of the event. I can't prove to you that God healed me after doctors said I was incurably ill, but I got better. You can't prove to me that the feeling of calm which took you through your

exams so that you did so well – after years of exam panic which made you do so badly – came from God.

There is no **empirical evidence** of either, in spite of how strongly convinced we each may be because of our own experience. This is the problem with religious experiences – they can't be proved, they can only be persuasive.

Sometimes a person changes radically after they claim to have had a religious experience. It's rather like Scrooge changing personality and behaviour after meeting the three ghosts in *A Christmas Carol*. They still can't prove the experience was real, but we can see the impact it had. Perhaps that will be enough to persuade us.

► *What reasons might a person give for believing a religious experience was real (whether it happened to them, or to someone else)? What reasons might they give for that experience having been an illusion (again, whether it happened to them, or to someone else)?*

A Personal, Life-changing Experience

There are many testimonies written by people who claim to have met God directly. This is known as *special revelation*, and is looked at again in Unit 4. Although it is impossible to prove the experience, the impact it has on the person involved can be so dramatic that other people believe it too. They can change completely in personality, behaviour, even looks.

One example is that of an American called Fred Ferrari. He got involved in petty crime as a youngster, and graduated to more serious crime as he got older. He was finally jailed for murder and, when locked up, was described by the prison governor as one of the worst people he had ever met. He even said that Ferrari would stay in prison until he died. In prison he was difficult to manage, and always ready to fight. One day a riot broke out and Ferrari was locked in his cell to keep him under control. Ferrari got angrier and noisier, cursing everyone. At some point, he began to curse God, as if God was responsible for all the trouble in his life. Ferrari claims God responded! The response was so powerful that Ferrari fell to his knees in tears. Later, he acquired a Bible to learn about Jesus and God. He began to work on the library trolley service and preach to other prisoners about how their lives could be changed by accepting Jesus. His words converted several prisoners and guards. He even had to have new photos done for his papers – his face had changed. Ferrari earned parole and release. He now spends his time travelling and witnessing about God's power and love.

I go to a local evangelical church. The services are very lively, and people are encouraged to let their emotions out, and to worship God as they feel is right. It's called charismatic worship. Having been a member for a few years now, I can quickly become very involved in the service. I invite the Holy Spirit to guide me and to work through me. I feel blessed by God's presence there.

The Basics

① What is a religious experience?

② State three ways in which people claim to have had religious experiences.

③ Define *reality* and *illusion*.

④ What reasons can we give to suggest religious experiences are
(a) real
(b) illusion?

Exam Tips

In this exam, you are expected to know simple ideas and to be able to show your understanding by application. Questions are often marked by the quality of your response – its breadth and depth. This means you need to give several reasons and explain them. Giving examples to back up your reasons shows a deeper understanding.

Simple Knowledge Questions

▶ *Write an account of a creation story from a religious tradition.* (6 marks) (AQA 1997)

Model Answer:

The Genesis creation story (1) is found in the Bible, which is the holy book of Christianity(2). In this story, we are told that God created the world in seven days from nothing. On each day God created something new to improve his creation. On day one God created light. On the next five days he created the firmament, the land, sea and vegetation, the sun, moon and stars, fish and birds, animals and finally man. On the seventh day, God rested. At the end of each day we are told, God saw that his creation was good.(3)

You can see that the religion is stated (2), the source of the story given (1), and the content outlined (3). The answer should get full marks. Try it with another creation story.

Levels of Response Questions

Remember – breadth and depth.

Explain why some people think the world is a 'result of chance'. (4 marks) (AQA 1999)

Model Answer:

Some people think the world is a result of chance because they don't believe in God (1a), so there is no reason behind its existence (1b). They may believe in the Big Bang Theory, which says the universe began when there was a huge explosion. This explosion came from nothing, but created all the matter which developed into the universe as we know it (2a). This was an accident, there was no God involved (2b). They may say that the world is chaotic, that there is no evidence of design. For example, so many natural disasters happen causing so much suffering, there can't be a God behind it all (3).

You can see that the answer gives three reasons – that's the breadth of an answer. Each one is explained. In (1), there is a reason (1a), followed by an explanation of why that point is important (1b). In (2), the theory itself is explained in depth (2a), and the relevance again shown (2b). In (3) there is an explanation and an example.

Try to do the same for this question.

▶ *Outline the argument for the existence of God based on design of the universe.* (AQA 1999).

Practice Questions

1 (a) What do we call a person who believes in God? (1 mark)

   (b) What do we call a person who doesn't believe in God? (1 mark)

   (c) What do we call a person who is unsure about the existence of God? (1 mark)

2 Explain the argument for the existence of God based on the origin of the universe. (4 marks)

3 Explain the argument for the existence of God based on what we know of
   (a) the human body
   (b) the natural world. (8 marks) (AQA 1997)

4 There are some reasons why God may not exist. Can you write down three? (3 marks)

5 Are religious experiences real or illusion? Give reasons for your answer. (3 marks) (AQA 1998)

6 Is it possible to believe in scientific theories of the origin of the universe and God? Explain your answer. (4 marks) (AQA 2000)

2 The Problems of Evil and Suffering

Twister hits Brighton

Man rips out girlfriend's eyes before murdering her.

Earthquake flattens city

More refugees flee Kosovan aggression

Old man mugged and left for dead

Flash-fires hit Florida

Flooded – 3rd time in two weeks

Cat loses tail in bonfire rocket attack

Pirates attack sail boat – two dead

Tortured – for £3.56

Bug epidemic hits harvest

These are all examples of bad news. You read things like this in the papers every day.

Put these headings into categories. Can you spot any similarities between them? Try to classify them in as many ways as you can.

Did you notice that some events can be blamed on people? Some are no one's responsibility. Some make us feel angry. Some are simply unfair. Some are downright cruel, or even evil.

We can split them up into two major groups. The first group are all natural events, they are part of nature. They result in pain for living beings, even death. We call this **natural suffering**, or suffering.

The second group are caused by humans – deliberate acts of unkindness, even evil, which cause pain to other beings. We call this **moral evil**, or evil.

Learn these terms, so that you give the correct answers.

We've Got Problems!

So, God is omnipotent, that means he can do anything at all. That's how he created the world.

And God is omniscient — he knows everything it is possible to know. That's like God knowing everything that everybody who has ever lived knows, and then knowing even more. Must have been really clever to design and make the world.

He is also benevolent — he loves us all. Loves each one of us, and wants us to be safe and happy. Like a perfect parent.

How come the world has got so much pain and trouble in it? Seems to me like God has a lot of explaining to do. He's powerful enough to stop it all; he knows about it all, and how to stop it; and he loves us enough to want to do something about it. So why doesn't he?

The person questioning God has looked at the big picture and seen the problems. Why does a God who is all-knowing, all-loving and all-powerful allow such pain and misery? The exam wants you to be able to break up that big problem into a number of smaller ones.

Read the passage below, and make a note of the problems it reveals.

I wish I hadn't read the paper today. All the news in it is bad news, just reminds me of some of the bad things happening around me. Is there any good around?

Take this story – a man ripped his girlfriend's eyes out with his fingers, before killing her a week later. He'd kept her locked up in between. What sort of evil is that? He even thought he was justified! Where do these people come from? What makes them like that? Isn't there anyone to stop it?

Here's another – an old guy was attacked in his own home. The burglars tortured him to get him to tell them where he kept his pension. They got away with £3.56. Terrible. He was an old soldier, and a decent enough chap. What had he done to deserve that?

Speaking of undeserved, what about the people of Bangladesh? Their country is flooded again. It happens every year to such a poor country. Thousands die, millions have to rebuild their homes and lives. They seem to get more than their fair share of trouble.

Then there's Montserrat – small island, big volcano! That's about to blow again. If I'd made the world, I wouldn't have designed so many places that are dangerous to live in.

There's a story about a kid who I know, because he's at my little brother's school. He's got some sort of cancer. That family have had it so bad this year. His gran died, and his mum was hurt in a car crash. Plus their holiday got ruined because there were hurricanes in the Caribbean – they'd saved for three years for that holiday. Surely it was somebody else's turn to get some bad luck? I know someone else in his school and they just get lucky all the time. They aren't even nice people!

My gran died the other week too. Now, she really believed in living a Christian life. She went to church regularly, gave money to any charity that asked for it, helped out for years at the church events, helped others who she thought were worse off than herself. In the end, she had three weeks of agony, after months of worry about what was really wrong, and what we'd do without her. What purpose did her suffering serve? It's not as if she needed her faith checking!

task

 Go back through the text. Make a list of all the questions you could ask about God.

 Split the list into questions about love, power, fairness, justice, evil and suffering generally. In the exam, your answers are stronger when you can give examples to back up the points you make. Try to give examples from the text to complete this task.

 Check the newspapers, and collect other examples. They are useful to use in the exam.

If you read this passage in a certain way, it raises many questions about God. These are often about God's power and how he chooses to use it; about God's love, who he loves, and how much he loves; about God's creation (the world) and its faults, including those present in humans; about God's sense of justice and fairness. Pain and suffering make us look at what God is supposed to be, and challenge it.

There are also general questions about God allowing moral evil to exist, or natural suffering to continue. Where does evil come from? Who is responsible?

These questions are major factors in the reasons given for not believing in God. We've all heard someone say 'Why me?' as if they believed someone was controlling their bad fortune. Some people see or experience too many instances of moral evil and/or natural suffering, and so give up their beliefs. Some see or experience too extreme an instance of moral evil and/or natural suffering, and so give up their beliefs. For some, the examples they see or experience simply give them extra proof that God doesn't exist. 'If God exists,' they say, 'God is not the God of any religion, but is uncaring, even **malevolent**.' With examples like the newspaper headlines, it's easy to see that view.

The Basics

①
What is the major problem linked to the existence of moral evil and natural suffering?

②
What specific problems are caused regarding
(a) God's love (b) God's power (c) God's creation?

③
Why do some people claim God is unjust?

④
What problems are raised for a religious believer by the existence of
(a) moral evil (b) natural suffering?

◄◄ Check out the information in Unit 1 about the world looking designed (p6). This topic brings that idea into question.

► Defending God

As a Christian, I believe that God is omniscient, omnipotent and benevolent. God's omnipotence makes his existence definite. I also know that there is much evil and suffering in the world. In the previous topic, we saw that there are many problems arising from these two points. So the question stands; Why does God allow evil and suffering? God created this world. God must be responsible for all the bad things that nature creates or causes. God is often described as a Father. Think about your parents. At times their action or inaction means you feel pain (physical, mental or emotional). Why do your parents allow you to feel that pain? Can you give examples to support your reasons? Christians have used similar arguments to defend God when challenged to explain why he allows suffering.

Case for Defence 1

All pain is a punishment for the things we do, say or think that are wrong.

Everybody does things wrong, and not everybody seems to get what they deserve for those things. So, the pain we feel through acts of evil and suffering is simply a punishment for our own badness. God is punishing us.

► Can you think of any examples which might back up this defence?

Case for Defence 2

Pain is a test of our faith in God.

The pain we endure is a test. In the Old Testament, there is the example of Job. Job's family is killed, his wealth lost, his animals and servants killed or stolen, his property is destroyed and his health taken away. Even his wife is fed up with him! This all happens in spite of the fact that Job is a good man, who worships God. These terrible events, which happened in quick succession, were a test of his faith. He passed the test and became rich again. If we view our own

misfortune and pain as a test, and we get through it, we will be rewarded by God.

► Can you think of any examples, which might back up this defence?

Case for Defence 3

All pain is part of an education for our souls. We learn from it.

We have to prepare for life in heaven with God. Pain teaches us the difference between right and wrong, appropriate and inappropriate behaviour, and makes us stronger. It also teaches us greater responsibility for ourselves, for others and for the world around us. We are learning to take care of what God has given us. Bad things happen when we don't take responsibility.

▶ *Can you think of any examples which might back up this defence?*

Case for Defence 4

There has to be badness for us to understand and appreciate goodness.

This means that we have the bad so that we recognise the good. There has to be a balance for either to exist.

▶ *Can you think of any examples which might back up this defence?*

Case for Defence 5

Evil and suffering are a result of free will.

Obviously, evil is caused by people making the wrong decisions. We were given free will by God. When it is our own choice, we can't blame God, can we?

What about suffering? Is that to do with our free will? It has been suggested that every action, thought and word has a positive or negative effect. These can be felt by us directly, or experienced indirectly, when they affect others. What if they create a force? The negative force will cause natural suffering to happen somewhere. If we change our behaviour, we can make a difference.

▶ *Can you think of any examples which might back up this defence?*

Case for Defence 6

Don't question God. Accept God's will.

We are only humans, and God is rather more special than we are. In fact, God is better in every way. God is **transcendent** – that is to say, God is beyond our understanding. We can't hope to understand God, so how can we understand what goes on in God's world. We can't see the big picture. So we should not bother trying to work out an answer to the problem – we were wrong even to pose it in the first place.

▶ *Can you think of any examples which might back up this defence?*

The Basics

①

Why do Christians need to defend God?

②

In what ways do Christians defend God? For each defence, give an example to demonstrate the point you make.

③

Do you think the solutions given here are adequate? Do they solve the problem of evil and suffering? Explain, giving reasons and examples.

Case for Defence 7

It isn't God who causes the evil and suffering. It's the devil.

When something bad happens, it's the **devil**, who is malevolent, causing it. Anything a person does, which is evil, is also caused by the devil, who is controlling them.

▶ *Can you think of any examples which might back up this defence?*

► **Focus on Evil**

Where does evil come from? How did it originally exist? What is it?

The Origins of Evil

If you read Genesis 3, you find the story of how Adam and Eve ate the fruit of the tree of knowledge. This made them see the difference between good and evil. They were thrown out of Eden (**Paradise**), and then made to take responsibility for themselves. The fact that they could now see the difference between good and evil – they could choose – meant that evil existed as a reality. So free will causes evil. God made evil possible by giving free will, but humans have actually created real evil.

► *So who is to blame — God or man?*

Satan

The **Gospel writers**, writing about Jesus, are the first in the Bible to suggest a devil existed. They describe the devil trying to tempt Jesus. The devil is named **Satan** (which is the Hebrew word for adversary). Thomas Aquinas, in the 11th century, suggested that this figure was actually a fallen angel. He claimed that one of the highest angels had become proud and challenged God. God threw him out of heaven, and he has opposed God on earth ever since.

► *Could this be the solution to the problem of evil?*

All in the Mind

Many people say evil is within us all as a latent force. If we are brought up in some terrible way, or our friends are themselves inclined to evil and so influence us, or we have some terrible experience in our lives, the evil within us can be triggered. So it isn't a force that overtakes us, it's something within – a psychological phenomena.

► *Can you think of examples to demonstrate this?*

An Impersonal Force

Some people see no organisation to evil. They see it as a part of nature. It is a negative force, which generates pain on a totally random basis. This may explain why not everyone reacts in the same way to their upbringing.

► *Does this explain evil adequately?*

The Basics

①
What is evil? How did it originate?

②
How are people themselves responsible for evil?

③
Evil is within a person and is not a power outside human beings. Do you agree? Give reasons and use examples in your answer.

► Keeping the Faith

You'd think people would give up on God. There is so much unnecessary, undeserved, unjust pain in the world, which God has the power and will to stop. God seems to be doing so little. So how do people – in their millions – keep their faith?

► *Can you think of anything positive which may come out of evil and suffering?*

When I am in trouble, or feeling low, I pray or read the Bible. It gives me comfort to know that God is watching over me. God supports me, giving the strength I need to get through.

Evil and suffering in the world give me the opportunity to show Jesus' love to others, and to live as a true Christian. It isn't just about words and beliefs –it's about spotting an opportunity to help, and taking it. We can all help in many ways — giving time, money, things . . .

I always approach troubled times and difficult experiences as times of learning. You know 'every cloud has a silver lining'. Well, I try to see the good in everything. There's always something to find.

I see my troubles as a test from God. I struggle, and overcome the problem. My faith is tested, but I become stronger through the test.

I know that God will help me through difficulties. God will not let me suffer too much. God will take away my pain, or will take me to be with him. I can still look with hope to the future.

The Basics

①

In what practical ways can a Christian help others? Think of five scenarios of people in need. Write the realistic ways in which Christians can help in each case.

②

How do people find their faith supports them through times of evil or suffering? Give examples to support your answer.

③

How do people find their faith is strengthened by times of evil or suffering? Give examples to support your answer.

My child died. I know she is with God in heaven. That thought really comforts me, because I struggled with her loss.

Who am I to question God? I must accept that God knows best.

Exam Tips

This topic has several areas of focus. Firstly, know what evil and suffering are. Secondly, know what sorts of problems they cause for believers. Thirdly, know what the solutions to the problem are (why does it happen?). Fourthly, know what the responses are (how people deal with it). You will also have to discuss statements from more than one viewpoint.

Practice Questions

1 Give an example of moral evil and natural suffering. (2 marks)

2 (a) What problems are raised for religious believers by
  (i) evil
  (ii) suffering? (8 marks) (AQA 1998)

  (b) Explain how pain and suffering can raise doubts about
  (i) God's love
  (ii) God's power. (6 marks) (AQA 1997)

3 Explain the teachings of one religious tradition about the reasons for either suffering or evil. (4 marks) (AQA 1999)

4 Explain how religious believers can respond in a positive way to suffering. (2 marks) (AQA 1999)

5 'Without suffering and evil, people would not turn to God or become better people.' Do you agree? Give reasons for your answer, showing that you have thought about more than one point of view. (6 marks) (AQA 1998)

Levels of Response Questions

Try to answer these questions before reading the model answers. Don't forget, the model isn't the *only* answer.

▶ *How might a religious believer explain why God does not stop evil and suffering?*
(4 marks)

Model Answer:

Religious believers might suggest that people do things wrong, so are being punished (1). They might say that it's a test of faith. God allows it to see how strong our faith is and to see if we will turn to God in this time of need (2). They might say that God is God – we shouldn't question why he allows anything. We won't be able to understand anyway because we are just humans, totally finite, whereas God is infinite (3).

There are three reasons given, each one more fully developed. The number of reasons makes half the available total marks probable; the development will give full marks.

▶ *Explain two ways in which believing in God may help a person who is suffering.*
(4 marks) (AQA 1997)

• They might *read their Bible to get comfort* from the words of God, because they feel God is close to them.

• They might *be hopeful that their illness will end* because God is looking after them, making sure that everything will work out in the end.

Read each answer. For each a reason is given (italics), which is then explained. When a question asks you to explain – do it! That's the only way to guarantee full marks. When you explain, don't just rewrite your reason – *They might hope their illness will end so it stops* – it has to say something else, it has to add to the original point.

3 The Nature of God

What is God like? What's your idea?

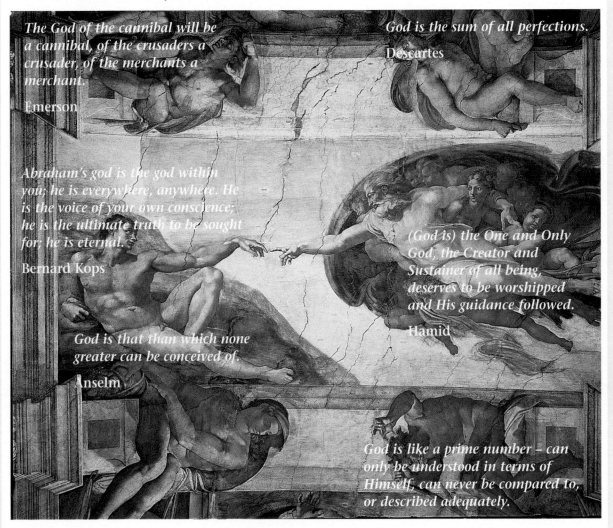

The God of the cannibal will be a cannibal, of the crusaders a crusader, of the merchants a merchant.

Emerson

God is the sum of all perfections.

Descartes

Abraham's god is the god within you; he is everywhere, anywhere. He is the voice of your own conscience; he is the ultimate truth to be sought for; he is eternal.

Bernard Kops

God is that than which none greater can be conceived of.

Anselm

(God is) the One and Only God, the Creator and Sustainer of all being, deserves to be worshipped and His guidance followed.

Hamid

God is like a prime number – can only be understood in terms of Himself, can never be compared to, or described adequately.

This Unit expects you to be able to describe ideas of God from two different religious traditions. You will have to understand specific words used to describe God, and the differences they create.

As you meet the definitions, ask yourself if they make sense? Is it meaningful to talk about God like this? Could we have a meaningful relationship with such a God?

► Religious Traditions of God

What Do Christians Believe About God?

The main **belief** of Christianity is that God expresses himself in the form of the **Trinity**. This is one God, but three forms. Forms or aspects are **not** individual gods. You need to know this difference.

In the **Apostles Creed**, we see an explanation of Christian belief. It includes descriptions of the three aspects of God – the Father, the Son and the Holy Spirit.

I believe in God the Father almighty, Creator of heaven and earth.

This is the first part to God – God the Father.

What does this tell us about God? Explain Father, almighty, Creator. Can we link any other characteristic to these?

GOD

And in Jesus Christ, his only Son, our Lord … crucified, died, was buried … rose again from the dead…will come to judge the living and the dead.

This is the second part – God the Son. God in flesh who lived on earth.

What does this tell us about God in this form? What shows him as special? What are his roles?

I believe in the Holy Spirit.

This is the third part to God – God's spirit on earth. It remains with us as a guide and support.

God is all three of these, they are all aspects of God. They each have different roles, but are still the same God. Think about yourself for a moment. Are you exactly the same when in school as you are when at home? What about when with friends? What about at a club you belong to? It goes on – we have different persona for the different situations we are in. We can use this analogy to help us to understand the aspects of God. God expresses himself in many ways.

What do Muslims Believe About God?

Say He is Allah the One. Allah is eternal and absolute. None is born of Him, nor is He born. And there is none like Him.
                    Surah 112, Qur'an.

One of the basic beliefs of Islam is *Tawhid* – the Oneness of God. **Allah** is the name of the Muslim God, it means *One God*. Allah cannot be split up in any way. Islam follows strict **monotheism**.

There are many names for Allah. The **Qur'an** lists 99 names, such as the merciful, the compassionate, the preserver. There is a story that there are 100 names, but only the camel knows the hundredth. It is just to show that we can never completely know God.

Allah is seen as the Creator of the Universe, which means Allah is all-powerful and all-knowing. Allah is eternal, which means he was never born and will never die. Allah does not change, because Allah is perfect. Allah is our guide through the Qur'an and the prophets.

three

What Do Hindus Believe About God?

Hindus believe in the Ultimate Reality, which they call **Brahman**. Brahman is eternal and unchanging. We can't understand Brahman, we can only understand parts and ideas of Brahman.

Brahman is split into three major parts – the *Trimurti*. This lets us more easily understand three of the major roles of God/Brahman. These are Brahma (Creator), Vishnu (Sustainer), and Shiva (Destroyer).

Hindus believe that the universe is in a continuous cycle of creation and destruction, then creation again. When it is time for the creation, Brahma has most influence and power, then Vishnu sustains the creation before Shiva is instrumental in the destruction. We can see this sharing of power on a lower level around us – seeds grow into plants  (creating), which live and flower/fruit (sustaining), and finally die (destruction), before rebirth after winter or through their seeds.

Hindus usually devote most of their worship to one of these three. They see that element as the most important, with the other two as lesser expressions of their chosen one. You can see an example of this in the Hindu creation story on p5 in Unit 1.

You may have seen statues or pictures of other gods. Ganesha, Lakshmi, Parvati, Durga are all children or consorts (partners) of the Trimurti. They are really just another way to understand Brahman, through the roles Brahman takes. You could research Hindu gods.

How can we understand this idea? Is it one God, or lots of gods? Imagine sitting in front of the TV. The picture is great from a few metres away, you can see the whole scene; it makes sense and you can understand what you are seeing. Now try sitting ten centimetres away. All you see are lots of dots of colour, which don't make sense, except in their own right. This is rather like the Hindu idea of God. We as humans don't have the capacity to see God in God's entirety, so we can only make sense of bits of God. So Hindus create gods of the bits of God, but they still all point to the One Reality of Brahman.

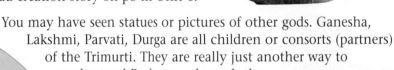

► One God – Many Gods – No God – Aspects of God

If I believe in one God, I am a *theist*.

If I believe in many gods, I am a *polytheist*.

If I don't believe in God or gods, I am an *atheist*.

If I don't think it is possible to prove or disprove the existence of God, so am unsure, I am an *agnostic*.

Some religions believe that one God can be split into different forms or aspects, for example, Hinduism and Christianity; others, like Islam, believe there is only one God who cannot be broken into elements.

Read the following statements. Which definition word from above is an appropriate label for each? You will need to learn the words for your exam.

I don't know whether there is a God or not. Sometimes I think there is, other times I'm sure there isn't.

God is all around us, in everything.

You can't prove God, so as far as I'm concerned there isn't one.

I believe there is a god for each one of us.

When someone proves God exists, then I'll believe.

A god of the moon, a god of the sun, a god of the trees – all forms of God.

God is here now.

God is a crutch for the weak to lean on.

There are different gods for every element of life.

God is nowhere.

Think about the religions on the previous pages. Which of the definition words on this page applies to each?

Over the next few pages, you will meet several other descriptive terms for God. Each time, check them against the two religions you chose previously. Get to know these ideas of God from your chosen religions really well. They will provide you with the examples you need in your exam.

► Immanent or Transcendent … or Both!

Immanent

When talking about God, this means God is involved in his Creation, active in the world. This is possible because of God's almighty power, and is a sign of his love for us.

► Why is God's immanence a sign of his love?

Jesus was an example of God's immanence. Jesus was God on earth, trying to show people the way to live and so to attain heaven. Jesus' ability to perform miracles was due to his divine status. This was God active in the world.

► Can you relate any of Jesus' miracles?

Many people believe that God makes things happen, which are naturally impossible, for the purpose of good. For example, a person is diagnosed with a brain tumour, which should kill them, yet it suddenly begins to shrink. When questioned, doctors can only say what it is doing, ie disappearing, not why. The person involved sees this as God's intervention.

► Do you know of any stories of modern day miracles?

Examples of people meeting God or having religious experiences are also examples of God's immanence. God has to be involved to be able to let people experience him.

► Can you think of any examples of people claiming such experiences?

Transcendent

When we talk about God as transcendent, we mean God is beyond this world and its limits. That doesn't mean God is far away – not in distance terms anyway. It means that God is distinct from the world. God is not controlled by time, so is eternal, never born and never to die. Nor is God limited by space, so has no physical qualities.

► What does this mean for any efforts to prove God exists by scientific means?

God does not need the world or rely on it, though the world needs and relies on God. This means that if God didn't exist, then neither would we.

It also means that we cannot ever hope to understand God because God is beyond our limited intelligence, which is exactly what you would expect of the being that created the world. Try comparing man's creations to that! This is why some people claim that we should not try to understand why God allows evil and suffering – we simply can't.

► What has man created that does the job of something natural? How good is it in comparison to the original?

The Basics

① What do *immanent* and *transcendent* mean?

② Make a list of reasons why people might prefer God to be (a) immanent, and (b) transcendent. What problems might each cause for religious believers? (Think of how people might feel to help you answer these.)

③ Can God be both immanent and transcendent? Explain your answer.

④ Can a human have a meaningful relationship with either? Explain your answer.

three

► Personal or Impersonal

Personal

If you have a personal relationship with someone, what does that mean?

It's about being close, about knowing someone, being able to speak with them and to confide in them. It's about knowing they are concerned for you and will listen to you.

When we say God is personal, we mean all those things about God. We can have a one-to-one relationship with God, and can experience God in our lives. We can each relate to God as a friend. God can have such a relationship with everybody at the same time because he is omnipotent.

► In practical terms, what would this mean in the life of the believer?

It also means we can describe God in human terms, even though God is clearly beyond human comprehension. This is how we can call God *Father*, or speak of him with human qualities (loving, forgiving etc.).

► Do you know of any other such expressions?

Impersonal

When we use this term to describe God, we are saying that we cannot relate personally to God, because God is God. We can worship God, though, as a sign of our acceptance of God's superiority. We can't describe God – our terms are inadequate for the vastness that is God. God is beyond our understanding.

► What evidence/ideas might a religious believer put forward to back up this point?

Impersonal also means that God is distant from us, because God is not like us in any way.

God's influence is on the world as a whole, not on our individual lives.

► Does this explain why evil and suffering exist?

The Basics

①
Explain the terms *personal* and *impersonal*.

②
Make a list of reasons why people might prefer God to be (a) personal and (b) impersonal. What problems might each cause for religious believers? (Think of how people might feel to help you answer these.)

③
Can a human have a meaningful relationship with a God described as either of these? Explain.

task

① You must learn these four words — transcendent, immanent, personal and impersonal. Can you spot which statement relates to each?
(a) Mr Smith says God is beyond our understanding, because we are human.
(b) This book says God is pre-existent — never born, never to die.
(c) The vicar says God came to earth as Jesus to die for us.
(d) She believes God is with her all the time, listening and concerned for her happiness.

② Try to make up more sentences which demonstrate each of the four words.

► Why the Different Ideas About God?

You may have noticed that different people in your class have different ideas about what God is like. In your earlier studies, you will have observed that religions speak of God in a variety of ways. Ever wondered why? Well, you need to know, because that very question might be on your final exam paper!

How People Learn About God

If I belong to one religion, and you belong to another, it's likely we will have different ideas of what God is like. Just check back to the page about ideas of God in three faiths (pp22–23) to see. How do they differ?

What we are taught in our places of worship, through holy books or teaching from religious leaders, will differ. For example, in the Qur'an, we see that Allah is totally beyond man's reach – transcendent. In the Christian faith, however, God is very much accessible – an immanent God.

I might also meet others who claim to have met God. They might show me an idea of God to which I have no access because of my faith.

Probably my first impression of God comes from my parents. Upbringing is our number one influence.

How People Experience God

People claim to have met God in various ways, and at various times. This will affect their understanding of God.

If I meet God when I am very unhappy (because of a tragic event, for example), I might feel that God is helping me through. I might see God as a caring, loving figure, who is very much active in the world. That idea would help me through the difficult time, and encourage me to pray more often. On the other hand, if I have done something wrong, and I meet with difficulties in my life, I might see these as punishment from God. In this case, I might feel that God is like a judge, and to be feared, so I worship him more strictly.

► Can you think of any more examples?

Personal Preferences

Maybe I just prefer one idea about God to another.

I look around the world and see much suffering and evil. How do I reconcile this with the existence of the God I worship? I could say God is transcendent, because that helps with my dilemma. It makes the whole problem easier.

Alternatively, I might want to follow a God who is active in the world, so I don't feel alone. Even in the blackest hour, there is hope, because God is by my side.

► Can you think of any other examples?

The Basics

① In what ways do people find out about God? List them, and give examples to show your understanding.

② Why might two people have different ideas of God?

►► See Unit 4 'General and Special Revelation'.

three

Exam Tips

This Unit is very dependent on words. You *must* know what these words mean: transcendent, immanent, personal, impersonal, monotheism, polytheism. Learn them.

You must be able to discuss why people might prefer one idea to another, why there are different ideas of God, and what problems are caused by believing in certain idea. You must demonstrate you understand the words. These questions rely on you picking out a *trigger word*, which gives the question its emphasis.

Practice Questions

1 *Explain why some religious believers prefer to think of God as 'immanent'.*

(2 marks) (AQA 1998)

What is the trigger word here? We need to know immanent, but this question isn't about definitions – it's about why we prefer that definition. It's about how much better that type of God makes me feel.

2 *What leads some religious believers to think of God as being in several forms rather than only one form?* (4 marks) (AQA 1998)

What leads is the same as saying *why*. It is important to answer that – to discuss which religions believe in one rather than the other can't get you full marks. Also, don't get confused with *several forms* – it doesn't mean *many gods*.

3 *If God exists, can a human being have a meaningful relationship with him?*

(6 marks) (AQA 1999)

If God exists demands you answer as if God does – *God doesn't exist, so you can't* isn't a valid answer. *Meaningful* needs to figure in your answer. It is a personal thing – only the person concerned can say something is meaningful to them.

4 *God cannot be both immanent and transcendent. That is impossible! Do you agree?* (6 marks) (AQA 2000)

This is asking you to compare two seemingly opposing statements about God. The mark value tells you that to get more than half marks, you must discuss two views – agreeing and disagreeing. It isn't enough to just say they are opposites – you need to demonstrate that by showing you know what each word means. You are going to have to move into other qualities of God to answer this easily. Do God's roles offer a solution? What about God's power? *Don't* get drawn into answering only about immanence or transcendence, such as asking how God can be immanent for everyone at the same time (easy for an omnipotent being which we don't understand really!). To look only at one descriptor and not the other doesn't answer the question – you are likely to get *no marks*.

4 General and Special Revelation

This Unit is concerned with how people learn about God, particularly through revelation. It is linked to the Unit on the Nature of God, because how we learn about God affects our idea of what God is like. It is also linked to the Unit on the Existence of God because it gives people personal evidence for God's existence.

Many people say they will only believe in God when they meet God. Maybe you are one of them. Think about this though – if you met God, could you prove it?

God is known through revelation (God revealing something of himself). There are two forms:

Special Revelation	**General Revelation**
Direct revelation, God communicating directly with you (as an individual or a group).	Indirect revelation, God revealing something of himself through other things, eg nature, people, events. Your interpretation leads you to say you have experienced God. That interpretation is based on a feeling.

Learn these. You may be asked to explain them in the exam.

Special Revelation

You have already met one example of special revelation (see Unit 1, p11). Do you remember the story of Fred Ferrari?

Events such as this are direct revelations – God comes directly to the person involved, and makes himself known. The event can have a massive impact on the life of that person – in Ferrari's case, it completely changed him. There is, though, no scientific evidence of the experience being true. We cannot prove it was real by scientific means. How can we demonstrate it was real?

Actually, if we can't prove God by scientific means, we won't be able to prove that someone did meet God, will we? All we can do is listen to their testimony and judge the impact it had on them.

For the exam, you may need to be able to describe special revelations from each of two religious traditions. You will see examples of these on the next page. When reading them think about the impact they had on the people concerned. What difference was made to their lives?

► If you had been either person, what would you have believed? Explain why.

► Would you say that this type of direct experience is the best evidence for God's existence? Explain yourself.

When someone has a direct special revelation, they feel they have met God in some direct, clear way. Maybe they have spoken to God, maybe they have heard God, or felt God's presence. Whatever happened, they are convinced this was God, and they know God through this meeting. These experiences can be life-changing.

The Conversion of Saul

This story is found in the New Testament (*Acts 9 v 3–7*).

Saul was a Jew and believed that Christians were blasphemers. Under Jewish law, this carried the death penalty. He made it his business to hunt down Christians, and have them executed. He was on his way to Damascus with some others, when he was blinded by a flash of light. As he cowered in the light, he heard a voice asking 'Why do you persecute me?' Saul enquired who was

speaking, and the voice identified itself as Jesus (who had died some years before). The now blind Saul was led into the city by the men who had heard the voice but seen nothing. He was taken to a house to rest for three days, after which time a Christian came to see him, and cured his blindness, having been instructed to do so by God. Saul (now with the new name of Paul) immediately converted to Christianity; having once been an enemy of the faith, he was now one of its strongest figures. In fact, Paul's teachings form the basis of much Church teaching today.

The Prophethood of Muhammad ﷺ

Muhammad ﷺ had taken to spending time in the caves outside Mecca meditating. He was confronted by a huge figure, who was later revealed to be the Angel Jibrail (Gabriel). This man, as it seemed to Muhammad ﷺ, ordered him to read. Muhammad ﷺ was illiterate – he could not read, and said so. The man squeezed him hard, so hard he thought he

would die. He did this three times altogether – demanding he read, then squeezing him. On the third time, Muhammad ﷺ recited the words – as if he knew them already. Muhammad ﷺ then realised he was alone, and went to the mouth of the cave.

Outside, in the sky, he saw the giant figure of the man flying. The man said he was Jibrail, and that Allah had chosen Muhammad ﷺ to be his messenger, to spread his word to mankind. A couple of months later, Muhammad ﷺ was again confronted by Jibrail, and he accepted his role as prophet. His whole life changed.

The Basics

① Define *revelation*.

② What is the difference between *special revelation* and *general revelation*?

③ Write accounts of two direct revelations of God and state which religious tradition each comes from.

► Knowing God … Through Nature

Nature is beautiful.

Nature is clever.

Nature is complicated.

It seems that there is design and purpose in nature.

These ideas provoke a sense of awe and wonder in many people.

► *Make a list of examples of how nature is each of these things.*

You have already seen these ideas presented elsewhere in this book. The idea of nature having been designed is met in Unit 1 (p6), and the idea of nature creating a sense of awe and wonder is part of what Otto discussed (see Unit 1 p11). Students should be able to see and use the links between Units and topics. Retrace your steps to reinforce your ability to answer on this topic.

Many people would say that the sense of awe and wonder they feel when experiencing nature is a sense of the divine on earth. It could be seen as evidence that God is immanent, because God is visible through his creation, or in the workings of his creation. This idea can be difficult to get your head round. Let's explain it in a different way. If you like art or music or film or books, you may like a particular person's work. There is something about their style, which draws you to them. Even when you haven't heard or seen or read their latest work, you might buy it. You can also recognise their work, because of the style. When you get used to their style, you may feel it tells you something about them as a person – their thoughts or feelings. Can you think of any examples of this?

This is very much how some people see the world – it is God's creation, and so is full of hints about God. Generally speaking, the world and nature are good – so God is good. The elements of the world, although we try to use the ideas and imitate them, are vastly greater than those we could devise. We could, therefore, say that God is much wiser, cleverer, and more powerful than we are.

► *Can I prove that whatever I feel is the correct interpretation of what I see? Can I use it to prove God's existence to anyone else? In other words, is it real or illusion?*

The Basics

①
How can we know God through nature? Give examples to support the points you make.

②
How strong a proof is nature for God's existence? Explain your answer.

③
How strong a proof is this for God? Could we ever prove it was real (or illusion)?

four

► ... Through Worship

There are three types of worship – Charismatic, Sacramental (or Ritualistic) and Contemplative. Read these accounts given by practitioners of each. Since worship often includes the use of holy books and teachings, there is some overlap into the next topic. However, there is also the feeling of a presence of God, perhaps that God is active in these events, as well. Does that mean we can know him better?

Charismatic Worship

When I was little my parents took me to the local church. Then at 18, I visited a Pentecostal Church, and was smitten by their services. The people in there were really free with their emotions and love for God. They sang and clapped and danced. To me it looked a little strange, and I must have shown it in my face. Someone took me aside, and explained to me that the people had welcomed the Spirit into their lives. Now they were praising God in a totally uninhibited way. God had accepted them, forgiven them, and was there for them. This sort of stuff is labelled the *fruits of the spirit*. You just have to open up to God, let him in, and do what he wants you to do. It is really spontaneous. It's also amazing to see people so happy, crying with happiness, people speaking strange languages that you instinctively understand, even people being healed at times. All of this is God working through them. Of course, there is a pattern to our worship, but each person reacts differently. It is as if God uses these people as his voicepiece to the world, and they are seeing him.

Make yourself familiar with how the different types of worship actually look in pictures. Previously it has been an exam task to identify types of worship.

task

① How can we define each type of worship from the descriptions given below? Look at the following three definitions. Which fits each type?

(a) This type of worship is quiet, often solitary. It involves focusing on some image or idea. The important elements for the believer are thought, focus and concentration.

(b) This type of worship is often very happy and lively. People do as they feel moved to do — for some that may mean singing, for others dancing, and so on. It is spontaneous. They let the Spirit of God work through them, granting the gifts of the Spirit.

(c) This type of worship is very traditional. It follows set patterns, and there is often an element of set wording to it. God's blessing can be received through this type of worship.

Sacramental Worship

I go to church every week. I always take part in the Bread and Wine service, which is at the end of our normal service, once a month. It's always the same, we sit at pews near the altar, and then go to the altar. We each get a piece of bread, which represents Jesus' body, and eat it. Then we are given a small glass of red liquid to represent Jesus' blood. We all drink this at the same time. The minister emphasises that Jesus gave up his life for the sake of our sins, so that we can go to heaven. Although it isn't really Jesus, I certainly feel blessed in some way, and refreshed in my relationship with God. Even though it's always the same, I always feel God's love and blessing anew.

Contemplative Worship

When I meditate, I always focus on a picture of the Creation. It's quite an old one that I found in a junk shop, but it had something about it. I try to visualise it in my mind, and, as I focus and concentrate, I feel a part of it. I feel closer to God because I am seeing his creation, and appreciating its vastness and wonder. This is a very quiet and still time for me and after it I always feel very refreshed. I

also feel that God has guided me through what is a healing time. I suppose it's like prayer in some ways, but I am alone, and it takes much more of my time and focus than I ever gave to prayer. What I still do that I did in prayer is to try and put my problems to God, and listen whilst he helps me to find answers. The quiet and focus is very helpful for this.

The Basics

① Define each type of worship.

② Describe elements of each type of worship.

③ How much can people learn about God from worship?

④ Is one type of worship better than the others? In what ways?

▶ ... Through Holy Books and Religious Writings

This seems pretty obvious – after all, holy books and religious writings are meant to be about God, aren't they?

Holy Books

So what do we learn about God from holy books?

The Qur'an gives 99 names for God. The Bible describes God in many ways.

The Torah gives the Ten Commandments, plus 613 **mitzvot** (laws). Qur'anic law forms the basis of **Shariah** (Muslim law).

The Old and New Testaments mention God in historical events.

The holy books are all about God, but these three elements stand out: what God is like, how God has acted in the history of the world to influence it, and how God wants us to live our lives.

We can look at holy books in many different ways. Indeed, their believers make different claims for them. The way we view a holy book will decide how closely we follow it, how we treat it, and how we understand what it tells us about God. Refer back to Unit 1 (pp4–5) to see explanations of different understandings of holy books. If I take a book literally, for example, I believe every word to be accurate, so my God will be exactly as described.

Religious Writings

How are these different from holy books? Well, they are the writings of religious people to explain what is written in the holy books, or their own experiences of God, or the teachings of their religious tradition.

▶ *Do we really need people to do this for us?*

Perhaps the most famous religious leader in the world is the Pope. Head of the Catholic Church, he has written papers about Church teaching. He is also said to be speaking the **infallible** word of God when speaking ex cathedra. Roman Catholics look to the teachings of the Pope for guidance in their religious lives.

Currently enjoying a high profile is the **Dalai Lama**, the leader of the Tibetan Buddhist faith. As Buddhism has gained in popularity in the West, so the Dalai Lama has become more and more famous. He is currently writing and publishing a series of books which try to put ancient Buddhist teachings into modern language, to make them accessible and readable for the West. In fact, one of his most recent publications, *Ancient Wisdom, Modern World* was top of the bestseller list for many weeks.

The Basics

①
What are holy books and religious teachings? Give examples of each.

②
What can we learn of God from these? Give examples.

③
How useful is either in helping us to know about God? And, how well can we know God through these?

four

► ... Through the Work and Lives of People

Some people, and the way they live their lives, make others think that God is at work in the world, acting through that person. This links with something you'll meet later in Unit 5 Ways of Making Moral Decisions – namely, that our beliefs affect our actions. However, it is more – it is that God is immanent through those people.

Persons X and Y follow a religion. What does this mean about how they live their everyday lives? Could we see something of God because they act out God's wishes?

Fred Smith values life because his religion says that everyone is special. He believes everyone is equal. This makes him treat everyone in the same courteous manner. It leads Fred to help those in need, because they are valuable too. He works with the down-and-outs in Manchester in a soup kitchen. Now, we could say that we can see God through Fred. Fred is doing what he believes God wants him to do: help others. We can also see that God is caring and loving, so we have learned a bit about God through that human.

► *Can you invent a character, like Fred, whose beliefs and actions can be taken as God working through a person?*

There are many people who have devoted their lives to helping others. That they claim to be led by God suggests God is loving and caring. There are many people who seem close to God. Some people are truly good people. They set examples, and we learn from them. Many of them claim God has spoken to them directly. We see God through their actions and words indirectly.

The Basics

①
How can we say that we see God through the words and actions of people? Give examples.

②
What does this tell us about God? What qualities can we see?

③
Is this a strong indicator of God's existence? Explain your answer.

Martin Luther King fought for and gained equal rights for black Americans. He was a Baptist minister, and believed God was using him to change America. His God was a God of love and peace, who called all men equal. Martin fought in a non-violent (peaceful) way. Find out about his work.

Mother Teresa believed that God had called her to help the poor and dying in Calcutta. She set up orphanages, hospices, clinics, schools and leprosy units for the poorest and least-cared-for of Indian society. She embodied the Christian teachings from the Parable of the Lost Sheep (*Matthew 25 v 34–40*) – that whoever you help, you help Jesus and God. Mother Teresa received a direct revelation of God, and herself became an indirect revelation of God.

four

► **Bringing Things Together**

You have seen a whole range of examples of special and general revelation. These all tell us some things about God and that we can know God. You do need to be able to think across the Unit though – not just that we can know, or what we can know, but also the reliability of what we can know. These questions come up in the earlier Units – is it proof of God to have met God? Can you prove God exists at all?

Are we really seeing God, or are we deluding ourselves? Can we explain religious experiences in any way other than God? If God is transcendent, can we expect to meet him? If we can meet God does that mean he can't be impersonal?

This page is designed to get you thinking about these questions. Look upon it as a sort of brain aerobics session!

I had been reading all about Saul, and later God came to me.

I only trust my gut instincts.

I'd believe anything she told me.

Choose the simplest answer and that's usually true.

She's my best friend. We went to primary school together.

If a tree falls in a forest, and no one hears it fall, and no recording is made, does it still make a sound?

> ► Do you know anyone? Really know them? How can you justify that answer?
>
> ► Do you think you could 'really know' God? Explain yourself.
>
> ► How well can you know God? What makes it difficult?
>
> ► Are revelations real or illusion? Which types of revelation are more likely to be real? Why?
>
> ► If I can't prove a revelation happened, did it happen at all?
>
> ► If I am religious, can you trust what I claim to have seen?

When I meet God, I'll believe in God.

If God's not physical, can we prove God?

There's got to be another answer.

How well do you know yourself? Do you really know how you'd respond in every situation?

◄◄ Check out Unit 1 (Meeting God, p10), Unit 2 (Defending God, p16) and Unit 3 generally.

four

Exam Tips

Simple Knowledge Questions

For this Unit you may be asked simple questions such as giving examples of revelation, or types of worship. Try these:

1 Give an example of sacramental worship.

2 State two types of religious experience people may have.

3 One way God has made himself known is through holy books. Name one.

4 What is the difference between general and special revelation?

It is likely that many of your marks will come from applying the ideas you have met. There is often some overlap into the earlier Units, too.

Levels of Response Questions

Let's take this opportunity to look at Levels of Response style questions for attainment targets AO1 and AO2. These are questions about knowledge and its application. The higher the level, the higher the mark awarded.

Levels of Response reward the depth and breadth of your answer, as well as its coherence, as follows –

Level One – a simple answer, often making just one relevant point. This is the sort of answer where you write the first thing that comes into your head and then move on. It isn't explained, or justified.

Level Two – if you gave a short explanation of that first thought, or gave an example of it, having stated it, you'd have pushed your mark into Level Two – you've

shown some depth of answer. At times, if you've given several simply stated reasons (no explanations or examples), you get Level Two – you've shown some breadth of answer.

Level Three – you need to give more than one reason, and to explain those reasons to get into this level, because it is about breadth *and* depth. Alternatively, you could give just one reason, which you have very clearly and fully explained.

Level Four – these answers need several reasons. A number of the reasons need to be clearly and fully explained. The whole response needs to flow in its style.

Try to answer the following questions, writing a response for each level to see how one level builds on the previous one.

1 *Explain why some people say that all forms of revelation are illusions and not real.*
(4 marks) (AQA 1999)

2 *How might a religious believer respond to the claim that God does not seem to be making himself known today?*
(4 marks) (AQA 1998)

In an earlier look at exam strategy (Unit 3, p28), we met the idea of answering the question set, and watching for trigger words. In question 2 above, don't talk about how right the statement is! Expect a religious believer to claim *God does make himself known*. The only way you could argue that they say God doesn't, is if you make a claim for God's transcendence.

four

5 Ways of Making Moral Decisions

This Unit underpins all of the remaining Units. The exam expects you to be able to discuss the attitude of different religious traditions to named issues, and to explain how they reached those attitudes. It won't be enough to say 'Roman Catholics believe abortion is wrong', for example. You'll need to be able to talk about why they say that and what teachings from their holy book inform that attitude.

Don't be fooled into thinking that religious people have a totally different agenda from everyone else. They do have particular books and people to turn to for advice, which non-religious people may not even consider, so you need to know about these. However, many of the reasons you might give for agreeing or disagreeing with something, they also might give. For the exam though, you do need to be able to state religious reasons for attitudes, if you want to maximise your marks.

Let's start thinking about **morality**…

► What does morality mean?

► Where do you get your ideas of what is right and wrong, what is acceptable and unacceptable? Can you make a list of sources?

Your morality is your sense of right and wrong, and you've probably written a huge list of sources, which help you decide. These sources might be internal to you (your conscience, for

example). They might be from people you associate with (parents, friends). They might be external ones forced upon you (the law, school).

Most people's idea of right and wrong changes as they go through life, and have new experiences and learn new things. Can you think of something you used to think was acceptable, and now don't – or vice versa?

We are all individuals, and our moralities may well differ, even if only slightly.

► Look at these issues. With a partner see if you share exactly the same attitude for each one.
Abortion; sex before marriage; marriage; divorce; adultery; racism; discrimination; world poverty; war; animal rights; vegetarianism; the environment.

Did you agree exactly on each? All of these topics are what we look at in this course. First we have to see what it is that shapes our attitudes.

► Absolute and Relative Morality

Absolute Morality

Someone who is an absolute moralist always follows the rules, which have been set (either by themselves or by external forces, like the law). They think that keeping the rules is the most important thing, no matter what the situation. The Roman Catholic tradition within Christianity, and the Muslim faith, are both examples of groups which follow an absolute moralist stance.

► *Can you think of any examples of absolute morality in action?*

► *Would you ever describe yourself as an absolute moralist? Give examples.*

Relative Morality

Someone who is a relative moralist always tries to judge a situation before making a decision. This means that sometimes the rules are broken, because that course of action does not seem to be the best one. Buddhism and most forms of Protestantism in Christianity are examples of relative moralist stances.

► *Can you think of any examples of relative morality in action?*

► *Would you ever describe yourself as a relative moralist? Give examples.*

The Ten Commandments

These are found in the Bible and are the basic rules of Christianity. They are a set of rules to live by.

Love God.

Do not make statues to God.

Do not take God's name in vain.

Keep the Sabbath holy.

Honour your father and mother.

Do not kill.

Do not commit adultery.

Do not steal.

Do not tell lies about others.

Do not covet anything that is someone else's.

task

Moral Dilemmas

We often find ourselves in the middle of a dilemma. Which option should we choose? How do we decide which to choose? Most of us use what we consider to be our own rules for life. We choose the option we feel most comfortable with, or which we feel is right. Look at the dilemmas here. Answer for each:

(a) What are the options?

(b) What would you decide, and why?

(c) If you were an absolute moralist following the Ten Commandments, what would your responses be?

(d) Are there any problems with taking an absolute moralist stance? Explain your answer.

① A 14-year-old girl is pregnant. Her family does not want to support her.

② A man is attacked. It seems his attacker is intent on killing him. How far does he defend himself?

③ You are asked to draw a picture of your idea of God, from which you will make a model.

④ You find a packed wallet in the street — it has a name in it.

⑤ Your friend is wrongly accused of graffiti in the toilets. You are scared of the one who really did it.

five

► Sources of Authority

Religious people have all the same influences as anyone else – parents, school, the law. Some influences they see in a different way – for example, you might see your conscience as your own mind, whilst an Anglican might see it as guidance from God. They do turn to some areas which non-religious people do not, though. Each religious tradition might have its own version of any of these. Each influence is a source of authority, because it guides and orders our decisions.

The Basics

①
Make notes on each source of authority. Use some of the words from the border to give examples of these sources. Link each to the religious tradition it represents.

Bible . . . Humanae Vitae . . . Pope . . Vicar . . . Apocrypha . . . Qur'an . . . Imam . . .

Hadith . . . Ijma . . . . Sunnah . . . Shariah . . . Torah . . . Talmud . . . Rabbi . . . Minhagim . . . Tipitaka

Guru Granth Sahib . . . Adi Granth . . . Vedas . . . Brahmin

Dalai Lama . . .

Scripture

This means holy books. These are perhaps the most important source of authority, because often they are seen as coming from God, either directly or indirectly. They are also the oldest sources in many cases. The holy book tells its readers what God is like, and how to live their lives.
Why does the strength of influence vary?

Tradition

This is extremely important in religions such as Judaism. It is a description of accepted practices and ideas, which go back many centuries, even to the beginning of the faith. These are like guidelines as to how certain things are done. The Jewish *Minhagim* are a series of such customs, and are inspired by devotion to God and desiring to do what God wants you to do.
Why should anyone keep tradition?

Reason

This is our intellectual ability to explore an issue, and come up with a suitable decision. Religious people often have to use this to work out how to apply the rules of their faith to a modern issue. Don't forget, the holy books are ancient, they don't mention every issue in our world today. Many religions actually write down this process of reason in books. *Why have a set body to do this? Why not do it ourselves?*

Conscience

As stated earlier, many religious people believe that our conscience is how God speaks to us. Your conscience is your moral sense of right and wrong. We often see it as a little voice inside ourselves.

Religious leaders

If anyone should be able to give advice, these people should. They have usually been trained to understand and interpret their holy books. Many are seen as specially gifted by God. Some even claim to have spoken to God. *There are different levels of religious leaders but are they all as reliable?*

Bible . . . Humanae Vitae . . . Pope . . Vicar . . . Apocrypha . . . Qur'an . . . Imam . . .

◄◄ Check out Unit 1 (pp4–5) looking at interpretations of holy books. Where a holy book is interpreted as the literal word of God, its contents will have a much stronger influence, and may even dictate people's actions.

► Beliefs – Values – Behaviour

► *Are the three words heading this page linked? Can you give examples to demonstrate your answer?*

Most of us live our lives by a set of values. The values may not be the same as those held by the country we live in, or our parents, or our school. We tend to keep to the rules within these contexts, even if we don't absolutely agree with them. These rules are based on values.

► *Think of your school's rules. What values can you see through these rules?*

If the values form the rules, then they must inform our behaviour. Think about it. Given a list of things to do, how do you decide which comes first? It's the one with the biggest priority usually – we put a value judgement on each.

For this course, you need to be able to show how the beliefs of a religious person affect their actions. The beliefs come from holy scriptures, and a religious person tries to live by them.

Look at the statements opposite. How would the speaker of each respond to any of these issues? War; world poverty; euthanasia; abortion; divorce; the environment; protest; prejudice; compassion; capital punishment; forgiveness; marriage; treatment of others.

Make sure you keep the link between belief and action in mind as you work through the ethical units of the course, and especially in the exam. A religious tradition's attitude to something is based on its beliefs – you must be able to discuss them both.

How is morality examined? Quite often it has been a part of a question set on other topics e.g., 'Name a source of religious authority a Christian might refer to when deciding on …' Actually, you are always demonstrating it in any ethical issue. It can appear as a question in its own right. Be aware of the difference between *relative* and *absolute* morality, and how a believer in either type might respond to moral dilemmas.

1	I believe that all life is special and sacred.
2	I believe God created the world for us.
3	I believe God loves us all as individuals.
4	I believe that we were made in the image of God.
5	I believe man is ruler of his own destiny.
6	I believe that it is right to win at any cost.
7	I believe that all people are equal.
8	I believe in non-violence.
9	I believe the wealth of the world should be shared more equally.
10	I believe I have the right to defend myself, whatever it takes.

6 Abortion, Sex, Marriage and Divorce

In the exam you must be able to discuss the attitudes of two religious traditions to each of the elements, which make up this Unit. Don't forget, religious tradition can mean either different religions (e.g. Buddhism and Christianity), or different denominations within one tradition (e.g. Roman Catholic and Anglican within Christianity). This is also true for all of the other morality-based Units.

In the last Unit you were shown that beliefs influence behaviour. This is an important idea within these Units. The attitudes of religious people to different issues are influenced by what they are told in their holy books and by other sources of authority (just as you are influenced by yours). It will be helpful to you in the exam to be able to discuss the teachings, which lead to attitudes and so to behaviour. Each time you read a quotation, try to work out for yourself what it means in terms of the relevant topic.

This Unit is underpinned by two major concepts – the sanctity of life (bringing in quality of life), and covenant (including commitment and responsibilities). You will need to be able to understand their meanings for your exam.

Start to keep a glossary of important words. As you work through the Units, you could add new words. You could even go back and pick words out from the earlier Units of the book. Since the exam does ask for definitions of certain words and phrases, and uses them frequently in its questions, a glossary will be a very useful revision resource for you.

Here are some evaluative questions. An evaluative question is usually the last part of any question. In the exam, if the question is worth 5–6 marks, it *must* be answered from two or more points of view. If it is worth 3 marks, one side can be enough (though it is easier to get more marks by considering more than one view).

Try to answer these questions now, then try again after you have studied the religious responses to each issue.

① 'Abortion is simply murder.' How far do you agree? Give reasons to support your answer.

② 'Sex should be within marriage; it is for the purpose of procreation.' 'How far do you agree? Give reasons to support your answer.

③ 'Marriage is a promise made for life before God and man, witnessed by all.' How far do you agree? Give reasons to support your answer.

④ 'Divorce is a necessary evil in modern society.' How far do you agree? Give reasons to support your answer.

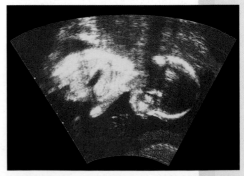

A fifteen week old foetus

► Abortion

This is the deliberate removal or expulsion of a foetus from a woman's womb, usually before it is able to survive independently. It is the deliberate ending of a pregnancy before term.

In Britain, abortion is illegal unless two doctors have agreed that certain circumstances are true. A woman may be granted an abortion if her own mental or physical health is at risk; if the health and well-being of existing children is at risk; or if there were strong indicators of physical or mental disability within the foetus. A woman must have an abortion before the twentieth week of pregnancy in most cases. Exceptionally, sometimes a woman may have to have a late abortion, because certain tests on the health of the foetus can only be carried out at a later stage, or she may become ill and her own health may be in danger later in the pregnancy.

► Why do you think some women decide to have abortions?

Throughout history women have had abortions. The British law was designed to protect women after it was realised that they would always break the law to obtain an abortion, regardless of the risks involved (even to their own health). It is a fierce debate though, which rages on today.

► Make a list of reasons why some people accept abortion, and some do not. Highlight any which are specifically religious reasons.

► Do any of your reasons show a concern for the sanctity of life? That is, how special, even sacred, life is? What about a concern for the quality of life (whose life)? That brings in the woman's right to decide the fate of her own body — has she that right?

Look at the following examples of women requesting abortion. Which ones do you find acceptable or unacceptable? Explain why in each case.

① A 14-year-old schoolgirl.

② A woman with five children already, who feels she and her family cannot cope.

③ A woman who has to have an operation to remove tumours from her womb – this will lead to the removal also of her womb. The operation is urgent.

④ A career woman, who does not want children, and who is pregnant because of failed contraception.

⑤ A woman who feels emotionally and mentally unable to have a child.

⑥ A woman who knows her child will be male, and who could pass on a congenital disease.

⑦ A woman who wants a boy, but is pregnant with a girl. Her husband agrees with her.

⑧ A woman with a severe learning disability, who lives with her carer.

As you made your decisions, those issues of sanctity and quality of life will have come up. It isn't such a straightforward topic, and that's why the religious traditions differ in their own attitudes.

► Abortion – the Religious Attitudes

Each section of quotations below belongs to a separate religious tradition. From each, try to work out a general attitude to abortion.

Christianity
Do not kill.

Exodus 20 v 13

You (God) formed my innermost parts, you knitted me together in my mother's womb … your eyes saw my unformed substance; in your book were written all the days of my life, before I even had them.

Psalm 139 v 13–16

When you (God) take away their breath, they die … when you give them breath, they are created; you give new life to the earth.

Psalm 104 v 29–30

Islam
Do not kill your children for fear of poverty. We shall provide for both them and you. Killing them is a serious blunder.

Qur'an 17 v 31

Those who have stupidly killed their own children without having any knowledge have forbidden something God has provided them with.

Qur'an 6 v 140

He is the One who has created you all from a single soul.

Qur'an 7 v 189

Sikhism
God sends us and we take birth. God calls us back and we die.

Adi Granth 1239

Those who love God, love everybody.

Adi Granth 557

This God is One … the Creator of all things.

Mul Mantra

You must have realised that religions believe life is God-given and God-taken. Does that give us the right to give or take life? Religions also believe that we are considered special because we are the creation of God. When does that creation take place? How does each affect abortion?

Let's look at some religious attitudes. As you read, think back to the quotes from above. They support the ideas given.

Roman Catholic View (Christian)

Abortion is *always* wrong. It is murder, because a foetus is fully human from conception. The *Didache* 'Do not kill a child by abortion' and other Catholic documents, such as *Vatican II* 'Life must be protected with the utmost care from the moment of conception' have condemned abortion throughout history. In cases where the life of the mother is at risk, e.g. ectopic pregnancy, or cancer of the uterus, the Church accepts the medical procedure, which also results in the ending of the pregnancy. This is called the Principle of Double Effect – it is not abortion. In terms of severely disabled children, they are still God's children – abortion is unacceptable, whereas the pregnancy gives us a chance to show God's love. Anyone who has an abortion, or who carries one out, can be excommunicated. This means that they will not be able to take the sacraments, and so are cut off from the daily life of the Church.

The Anglican View (Christian)

The Church believes in the idea of sanctity of life, and of God's creation of each of us, but sees abortion as a necessary evil at times, e.g. in the case of rape or threat to the health of the mother. It sees abortion as a procedure, which should not be taken lightly – only after the most serious moral reflection. Although it is needed, it is seen as an option too lightly taken by many. The Church urges better education to promote understanding of human sexuality and relationships, and recognises that the Church should get more involved in the moral and spiritual support of society to reduce the need for abortion.

The Islamic View

Many believe that a foetus is a life from the point when it acquires a soul, which is thought to happen at the end of the third month of pregnancy. Thus it should be possible to have an abortion before that time. However, children are seen as gifts from God, and should be accepted. All life is thought to be part of God's plan. So to have an abortion is a sin. When the mother's life is at risk, many believe abortion to be a necessary evil, but there are fundamentalists who believe it should be left to God to decide what happens.

The Sikh View

Abortion is *always* unacceptable. It is a grave sin. God has created each of us individually, and has a plan for each one of us. Clearly abortion is a rejection of both ideas. You could even say we are inferring we know better than God. Sikhs do not believe severe disability is an acceptable reason for abortion, though rape might be. Sikhs do, however, defend the right of a couple to decide for themselves.

The Basics

What is abortion?

Choose two religious traditions. For each, outline their attitude to abortion, using quotations to back up what you say.

③
Go back to p43, where eight examples of women wanting abortion are given. For the two religions you have chosen in Q2, state whether they would agree or not, and explain why.

Time Test
Give yourself 20 minutes to answer these questions without your notes.

① A pregnant woman has been told that she will have a severely physically disabled child, and should consider an abortion.

  (a) Explain why believers in one religious tradition are against abortion in this situation.

  (b) Explain why believers in a different religious tradition may think this situation justifies abortion.

② State and explain two other circumstances when abortion is regarded by some religious believers as acceptable.

③ If a baby is not wanted by its mother, there are many who would adopt it. It should not be killed. Do you agree? Give reasons, showing you have considered more than one point of view.

SIX

► Sex!

married

Definitions

Celibacy – not having sexual relations

Chastity – keeping oneself sexually pure

Adultery – having sexual relations with someone other than your spouse

This section looks at celibacy, sex before marriage and adultery. You need to know about the attitudes of two religious traditions. Since the teachings interconnect, we'll look at the topics via the faiths.

Generally Speaking

Celibacy and chastity are expected of anyone who is unmarried in most religious traditions. Although we may live in a society where people are almost encouraged to have sexual relationships without being married, most religious traditions hold to the notion of *saving yourself* for marriage. Why do you think they do that? What reasons could be given for and against not having sex before you get married? Don't forget, sex before marriage can be in the form of a relationship or casual sex (one night stands) – the two are different, and are viewed differently.

So why do we have sex? The answer to that will vary. There are probably many reasons, and at any one time, one reason may be more powerful than another. The answer will certainly influence our attitude to sex, as you will see in the religious views.

Why is adultery wrong? It isn't illegal in Britain, but it is a certain reason for divorce to be granted, so it must be wrong. Adultery is usually seen as a matter of betrayal; it can destroy a relationship.

a couple

Roman Catholic View

'Every sexual act must be within the framework of marriage.' (Casti Conubii, Catholic Truth Society). Only married couples should have sex, and then it should be primarily for the purpose of having children. One of three questions asked at a marriage ceremony is whether the couple will accept children. The use of artificial contraception is forbidden by the Catholic Church. For many practising Catholics, though, the teaching is not followed. Why do you think this is?

not married

All forms of sexual activity outside marriage are condemned as being wrong – even if someone looks at another person lustfully, they have done wrong *(Matthew 5 v 28)*. In the Catechism (the essential teachings of the Catholic faith) people who have sex outside marriage are classed as fornicators. From this you can tell that celibacy is expected of any unmarried person. You can also tell that adultery must be wrong. In the Bible, it says 'Do not commit adultery' *(Exodus 20 v 14)*; this is one of the basic rules direct from God. Thus, a couple, whilst apart, should remain chaste.

The Church of England View

The Church sees sex as a gift from God ideally to a married couple. However, it also sees the reality of modern society, and accepts that many couples will have sex before marriage. It condemns sex outside of relationships i.e. casual sex. This degrades sex, which is seen as the ultimate expression of love between two people in a permanent relationship. A major difference from the Catholic view, this highlights the shift in terms of how sex is viewed from being about having children to showing love. Looking at it like that, we can see that adultery would not be a loving act (towards your partner), and would be a betrayal of the wedding vows. It is seen as wrong.

just met

The Muslim View

'The only way to protect all within society is to maintain a society where only a man and his wife share the act of sex' (Islam – the Natural Way). The message is very clear in Islam – only married couples may have sex, and then only with each other. Prophet Muhammad spoke of sex as being special within marriage, and a source of pleasure. He also said it could provide the blessing of children from God, if the couple so wished. The Qur'an details specific punishments for those who have sex outside of marriage. These people are named as fornicators, and punishment is severe – the fornicator should be flogged if single, executed if married (Qur'an). In several places, the Qur'an specifically mentions adultery – it always says it is wrong: 'Do not commit adultery. It is shameful and an evil way to act' (Surah 17 v 32).

a couple

The Sikh View

Sikhism also states that sex should be enjoyed only within marriage. It is natural but special, and sex outside marriage degrades it. Many Sikh practices try to reduce the temptation to have sexual relations without being married. Sikhs are not allowed to dance with the opposite sex, or to do anything which might influence their behaviour in that way – 'Avoid that which … produces evil thoughts in the mind' (Adi Granth). Since Sikhism accepts the use of contraception, you can see that sex must be more than an act to create new life. It is seen as strengthening the bonds between a couple, and a symbol of the love they share. Adultery is always wrong. It is a betrayal of your partner, and shameful to your whole family. It is an accepted reason for divorce in Sikhism.

The Basics

Define the words – *celibacy*, *chastity*, and *adultery*.

Choose two religious traditions. For each explain their attitude to each of the three elements – celibacy and sex before marriage; sex within marriage; and adultery. Use quotations to back up your explanation of each. (It may help to refer to the topic of contraception.)

③
Sex should be within marriage – a committed, lifelong union. Do you agree? Give reasons and explain your answer.

Check out the section on ▶▶ Contraception, p48.

► Contraception

People use contraception mainly to protect themselves against pregnancy. For some, there is a need to protect themselves or their partner against disease (for example, if someone was HIV positive, but their partner was not, or if one of the couple was the carrier of a hereditary illness which they did not want to pass on to their future children).

Attitudes to the use of contraception vary amongst the religious traditions. First, let's look at the options. With a partner, list the types of contraception that you know of.

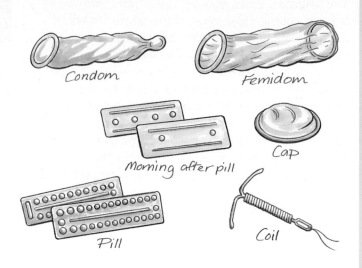

Condom

Femidom

Morning after pill

Cap

Pill

Coil

How Do they Work?

Some contraceptives block the sperm and egg, which then never meet. These are barrier methods, such as the condom, cap (diaphragm) or femidom.

Some ensure the woman menstruates, so that even if the egg has been fertilised, it won't be able to develop because it is lost with the menstrual blood. The coil (IUD) works like this, as does the morning after pill.

Some stop the woman from producing the egg at all, by introducing certain hormones into her system. An example of this is the pill.

Some forms are permanent. Men and women can be sterilised so that they are no longer able to cause pregnancy or become pregnant.

► *Can you think of any other methods, not mentioned above?*

Some people do not use artificial methods of contraception. The ones spoken about above are all artificial. *Natural Family Planning* is all about the woman learning about the cycles of fertility and infertility within her own body. It relies on her knowing when she can and can't get pregnant, based on close observation of herself.

The withdrawal method is perhaps the least safe method of contraception, but it is widely used. It relies on the man withdrawing from the woman before he ejaculates.

It is unlikely that you would be asked about types of contraception and how they work in the exam. However, you need to be aware of the information, because how they work is often the key to which religions will allow their followers to use them.

The Roman Catholic Viewpoint

There is no direct comment from the Bible. Catholic teaching in this case is spelt out in the encyclical *Humanae Vitae*, which was published in 1968. It stated that the primary reason for having sex was to have children. Every act of sexual intercourse should be open to pregnancy. This teaching came from the Catholic idea of *natural law*. Artificial methods were condemned as sinful, and against God (any action specifically intended to prevent procreation is condemned). As a result of this, Catholics are instructed to use only natural methods of birth control. Couples should have children, because this is one of the purposes of marriage.

'God said to Adam and Eve: Be fruitful and increase in number.' *(Genesis 1 v 28).*

In reality, many Catholics use contraception, and follow their own judgement on this issue. Do you think this is a problem for the tradition?

The Anglican Viewpoint

The Anglican Churches' view on contraception is quite different from that of the Roman Catholic Church. In the 20th century, at most Conferences to discuss Church teaching, the issue has come up. The Lambeth Conferences, when discussing the matter, have emphasised the duty of responsible parenthood. In other words, a couple should take precautions to have only as many children as they can properly bring up. Children are seen as a blessing to a marriage, but one that can be accepted when a couple feels ready and able. As to which type of contraception can be used, the Anglican Church sees no difference between artificial and natural – they both try to do the same job, which is to prevent pregnancy.

The Jewish Viewpoint

'God made the world ... He did not make it to be chaotic ... He created it to be inhabited.' (*Isaiah 45 v 18*).

The earlier quotation from Genesis is also accepted by Jews. So it is Jewish belief that couples should have children. Many Jews believe that God blesses them with children, so the greater the family, the greater the blessing. Some Jews (Orthodox) see using contraception as interfering with God's plan, so they don't agree with it. Reform and Progressive Jews accept the use of contraception, although many believe that they should have a minimum of one son and one daughter to fulfil the Genesis commandment. It is seen as sensible to use contraception in cases where the health of the mother would be at risk in pregnancy, or where an extra pregnancy would cause hardship to the family.

Permanent methods of contraception aren't accepted though – this is seen as mutilating the body. When you consider that you were created uniquely by God, it is wrong to damage yourself in that way. Although Orthodox Jews are often seen as very strict and maybe even old-fashioned, because they don't change their behaviour to suit society, the favoured form of contraception is actually the pill. The pill is taken by the woman, it doesn't interfere with the actual sex act, and it isn't permanent.

The Hindu Viewpoint

Hindus believe in reincarnation, so each foetus is a reincarnated soul. In each lifetime, we must try to learn and to purify our souls. Causing suffering is wrong, and will result in problems for our own souls in the future. If a couple brings a child into the world into a situation of suffering, maybe because they cannot afford to give it a good upbringing, that is a bad thing. As a result, most Hindus will limit the size of their families by using contraception. There is no religious teaching about what type, though. It is unlikely that Hindus would use permanent forms, unless there was a medical need. The religion demands a son for the carrying out of certain important rituals. So Hindus should have families, but the size and timing of them is up to the couple.

The Basics

① Name four methods of contraception and say how they work.

② Why do people use contraceptives?

③ What is the attitude of two religious traditions you have studied to the use of contraception? Try to use teachings and examples to back up your answer.

You are the Doctor

The following couples come to see you. They want contraceptive advice, but all have set beliefs, which may affect what you can say. Try to recommend a suitable contraceptive method to them.

(a) A Roman Catholic couple

(b) An Anglican couple

(c) A Hindu couple

(d) A Jewish (Orthodox) couple

Explain your recommendation each time.

It will help you to read the section on Sex and on Children (p50) as both contribute to the decision on which contraceptive method is made. ►►

SIX

► **Considering Marriage**

Ask most primary school children what they'll do when they grow up, and you'll probably get the answer – Get married and have a family. Even in our society where marriage breaks down so frequently, people still have this idea of being married.

► *Why do people marry? List all the reasons. Compare your list with a partner's.*

There must have been quite a few on your joint list – emotions, needs, wishes, ability to provide, means to an end – good reasons, bad

reasons. It's a big list. Were any religious? Of course, religions expect their followers to marry, and of course most of their reasons for marriage are the same as any non-religious

person's. However, there are some reasons, which are specifically religious. Can you think of any?

Why Do Religious People Marry?

Perhaps the first is that it is a duty or expectation within their faith. In the Hadith (sayings and deeds of Prophet Muhammad), Muslims are told 'Marriage is part of my example, and whoever disdains my example is not one of me'. In fact, there is no such thing as monasticism in Islam, and it would be unheard of for a Muslim religious leader not to be married. In *Genesis 2 v 24*, Christians and Jews are told that a man shall leave his father and mother, and cleave to one wife. For Sikhs, marriage is seen as the natural way, what God intends for all. In the wedding ceremony, there are a number of quotes from the Sikh Gurus showing that – Your God has designed you to unite with your partner.

► *Is this like peer group pressure since it influences peoples' lives and behaviour?*

A second reason is for sexual relationships and for children. Not all religious traditions believe that married couples must have children. They do all believe that God blesses marriage with children, though. The topics Sex! and Contraception both discuss these ideas. The act of marriage is seen as legitimising sexual relations, and keeping sex as a special act of love.

► *Why do most people feel that children should have a mum and dad who are married?*

A third reason is to continue the faith. Some religious traditions insist their followers marry people of the same tradition; this is so for Sikh and Muslim women. It is understandable that people fear their religion will be weakened if someone marries out of the faith. Why should non-Catholics take their children to Confession and Mass, if they themselves don't believe in it? Upbringing is a very strong reason for having a faith in the first place. If you think your faith is the true way, you won't marry out. When two people of the same faith marry, they can encourage and support each other's faith, and their children will also follow it.

► *How similar is this to the idea of shared attitudes, which many non-religious people look for in their partners?*

The fourth reason must include that marriage provides a loving partnership within which two people can support and help each other. This overlaps with the idea of keeping the faith, but is much more. The vows made at some marriages point towards this.

► *How might a faith help a couple in keeping their partnership as loving and supportive?*

A Commitment Being Made

Christianity stands out as having vows, which are made by each partner to the other. The vows are a statement of their commitment to each other. They are an agreement made between two people in the presence of many witnesses, and God. Marriage is a covenant, that is, a binding agreement, a contract. When couples sign a marriage certificate, they make this a legally binding agreement.

The vows, or promises, speak of looking after each other through good and bad times, good and bad health, until death. The couple are announcing their love and commitment to this union. They are saying that they will work to keep the marriage together, and to support each other. That commitment has given them responsibilities.

► *What responsibilities do you think marriage brings?*

The purposes of marriage point us towards some of the responsibilities, and the vows will point us to others.

► *Do you think that religious people's ideas of responsibilities will be the same as, or different from, those of non-religious people?*

In Christianity generally, the couple share responsibility for all aspects of the marriage, though some see the man as the head of the household, after the teaching of St Paul. Decisions should be taken together for the good of the family. Although both men and women work, the woman often takes the greater share in the upbringing of the children. Both share the role of guidance and discipline, as well as helping the faith of their children.

In Islam, men and women have different, but equal, duties within marriage. The man deals with the outside world, and provides financially for the family. He takes on the religious education of his sons when they are old enough to go to the mosque. The woman has responsibility for the home and for looking after the children. The Qur'an says that a man and his wife are like garments for each other; in other words they should comfort, help and support each other.

The Basics

① Why do religious people marry?

② How is marriage a covenant?

③ What are the marriage responsibilities for religious couples?

► **Who to Marry**

What do you look for in a partner? Are there certain characteristics and qualities you want your future partner to have? Why?

You probably included ideas about shared interests and attitudes, looks, general compatibility. Did money come into it? Or job prospects? What about how much your parents approved of your choice? What if any of those don't match up?

When we choose a partner, or find Mr or Ms Right, we have to be very sure, because the commitment we are about to make is massive, and brings many responsibilities.

Religiously Speaking

All religions prefer it if parents approve of their child's future husband or wife. Christians follow the Ten Commandments, one of which is to honour your father and mother. This might be taken to mean that you seek their approval in marriage. In the ceremony, the father traditionally gives away the bride, so he must approve of who he is giving her to.

Some traditions actually go further and expect parents to find a suitable partner for their children.

► *How would you view the idea of your parents finding a suitable partner for you?*

If you come from a culture where this isn't the norm, you might find the idea unacceptable. Why is that? Surely our parents would only want a partner for us who is the best – who will support and help us, look after us and make us happy.

In Sikhism, Hinduism and Islam, it is the usual practice for parents to find a suitable partner for their children. This is called *arranged marriage*. It is much misunderstood generally in the West, so let's look at the idea.

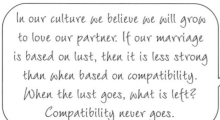
My parents found a person who is suitable for me in every way. He shares my interests and ideas, as well as my faith. His family and mine will get along because they are from the same sort of background. He is healthy, and has good job prospects, so will be able to provide for me.

I found it easy to get on with the girl my parents chose. We immediately felt comfortable in each other's company.

In our culture we believe we will grow to love our partner. If our marriage is based on lust, then it is less strong than when based on compatibility. When the lust goes, what is left? Compatibility never goes.

We met three times, and agreed to be married.

I did not feel the first person was right for me when we met. My parents respected my decision to say no, and began to find another suitable man.

SIX

So, arranged marriages are marriages where a suitable partner has been found by parents, or people acting on their behalf, for their child (when they are old enough to marry). The potential couple meet, whilst chaperoned, perhaps several times, and decide whether or not they wish to marry. If they do not, that wish must be respected. When they marry, they expect their compatibility and the support of both families will help them to come to love. By working hard at the marriage it is believed it will be a success. In countries where arranged marriage is the norm, divorce rates are much lower than in the West, which suggests that this sort of marriage works.

Same faith? Same race?

People from religious traditions are most likely to want to marry others from the same faith. Why?

Imagine believing that it is wrong to use artificial contraception, and your partner being fiercely against having children. That wouldn't work. Religions give us sets of values as well as rules by which to live our lives. As a result it is easier to marry someone who shares these values. Some religious traditions insist their followers marry those of the same faith, or marry people who are converting to the faith, e.g. Islam, Orthodox Judaism, Sikhism. Some forbid certain marriages, e.g. Islam forbids marriage to any other than Muslim, Jew or Christian.

In terms of the race of your partner, all religions believe all people are equal. There should be no room for prejudice against someone because of their colour. If there is, it is not because of the faith, but a human failing. Of course, marrying someone from another culture, which racially mixed marriages can be, can give extra difficulties to marriage. There might be totally different ways of doing things, or of responding to things. The couple might have to face prejudice from others. No religious tradition has a rule about not marrying someone of a different culture – only about not marrying a different religion (which may or may not be a different culture).

The Basics

①
What is arranged marriage?

②
How does arranged marriage work?

③
Why might religious traditions, which do not have arranged marriage, prefer the approval of parents in the marriage process?

④
How might mixed faith marriage be viewed by followers of a tradition where arranged marriage is the norm?

⑤
Marriages have to last longer than the initial attraction, that's why arranged marriage is better. How far do you agree? Give reasons and explain your answer.

◄◄ Check out the Section on Considering Marriage in Unit 6, pp 50–51 for more ideas on marrying someone of the same faith. Also check out Unit 7, Prejudice and Discrimination (p58) about attitudes to other cultures.

SIX

► Divorce

Divorce is the legal dissolution of a marriage. Current figures suggest that more than one in three first marriages ends in divorce in the UK.

► *Why do marriages fail? Are there any reasons you find more or less acceptable?*

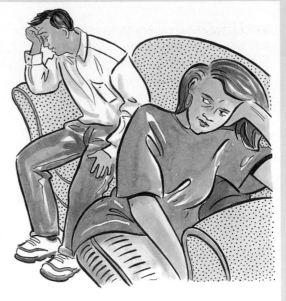

When Divorce Looms

Religious traditions view marriage as a very special, even sacred act. None wish to see marriages end, and so encourage the couple to work at their marriage. The initial commitment made, with its related responsibilities, is not to be taken lightly.

► *What options are there generally in society to help when marriages meet difficulties?*

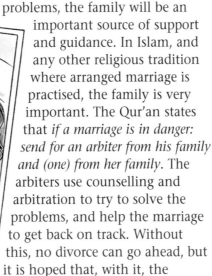

Apart from the efforts the couple might make to sort out their problems, the family will be an important source of support and guidance. In Islam, and any other religious tradition where arranged marriage is practised, the family is very important. The Qur'an states that *if a marriage is in danger: send for an arbiter from his family and (one) from her family*. The arbiters use counselling and arbitration to try to solve the problems, and help the marriage to get back on track. Without this, no divorce can go ahead, but it is hoped that, with it, the marriage will be saved.

Other people, who attend the same place of worship, may act in the same way for a couple. This can be true for Christians, who might also pray for God's guidance and support for the couple.

The religious leaders, maybe a priest or a vicar, can give the couple advice and listen to them. They will be mediating and counselling to try to see a way forward.

The couple may even be encouraged to separate temporarily.

► *How might each of these ways prove helpful?*

Attitudes to Divorce

'For I hate divorce, says the Lord God of Israel.' (*Malachi*)

'The lawful thing that God hates most is divorce.' (*Qur'an*)

Until death us do part (*Christian marriage vow*)

In many societies, divorce is considered so unacceptable that couples are forced to work out a solution to their problems, or live with them.

Roman Catholicism does not recognise divorce. Marriage is a sacrament, and is for life. A couple can have their marriage annulled or dissolved if they can show that certain things are true: if one was forced into marriage; if the couple never had sex within the marriage; if one partner could no longer do what was required of them in the marriage (e.g. had become mentally ill); if their intentions differed (e.g. one wanted children, the other did not). Annulment means that the marriage bond did not exist, for certain reasons there was never a real marriage. For a couple who are both baptised, then only annulment is available; for those couples who include one baptised person, it is dissolution.

▶ *Can you think of any reasons for divorce which are not included in the reasons for annulment?*

The Church of England was instrumental in getting divorce law changed in the UK in the late 1960s. Before then, there had to be some blame shown. The Church helped to change the issue to irretrievable breakdown of marriage. Although the Church sees marriage as a sacrament, and a holy estate, which should properly last for life, it accepts that this isn't always realistic. The Church encourages couples to try to work at marriage, and vicars will counsel the couple. As a last resort, the couple will divorce. Many Christians point to Jesus' requirement for us to forgive each other, and to the general idea that God gives us another chance after sin, to support their belief in divorce.

▶ *Why do you think the Church campaigned to change divorce law, when it doesn't support divorce?*

Buddhists do not have religious marriage ceremonies – they are social contracts. Their view on divorce is quite clear though. If a couple has tried everything, and realises there is no future to their relationship, and that they will suffer to continue in it, they should seek divorce. It is considered wrong to force people to stay in situations of suffering, just to promote an ideal. For a number of couples, divorce is the only compassionate solution, and compassion is the Buddhist way.

▶ *Do you think people in the West look upon divorce in this way?*

Islam considers divorce to be the very last resort. It is acceptable, but not wished for. The family of a couple have a great obligation to work to prevent divorce, but even they can fail. At those times, divorce is available quickly and easily. Not many divorces happen though – Islamic society isn't used to divorce, and so peer pressure works against it.

▶ *How difficult do you think it would be to obtain a divorce in such a society?*

The Basics

① What is divorce?

② Why do people get divorced?

③ Choose two religious traditions. For each, discuss how followers might try to help a couple with marital difficulties.

④ Explain the attitude of two religious traditions to divorce.

⑤ Divorce is an easy option for those not really committed. How far do you agree? Give reasons and explain your answer.

SIX

Exam Tips

There have been many different topics raised in the questions in this Unit. You have to know definitions of words, reasons behind choices, religious teachings on issues and their origins, how those beliefs affect the lives of believers. Some of the topics have not been obvious, and so you need to see the linked issues.

The final part of most questions in the exam will be an evaluative question. This has its own Level of Response criteria, with five levels. They are usually worth 5 marks. They are phrased quite particularly (e.g. give reasons for your answer, showing you have thought about more than one point of view), and to gain more than three marks, you usually have to answer from two or more points of view. The levels can be described as follows:

LEVEL		
Level One	1 mark	Simple justification – ***I agree because...***
Level Two	2 marks	Opinion supported by one elaborated reason, or two or more simple reasons (for same or different points of view) – ***I agree because of... and...***
Level Three	3 marks	Opinion supported by one well-developed reason or two elaborated reasons – ***I agree because..., which means ...***
Level Four	4 marks	Two distinct points of view, each explained or supported; there has to be evidence of reasoned consideration, i.e. perhaps including examples and quotes as support – ***I agree because... Others might disagree because...*** (plus explanations).
Level Five	5 marks	A clearly and fully explained answer, which gives good balance and weighting to both sides of the argument. Will include quotations and examples to fully develop the points being made – ***In some ways I agree for these reasons..., for example..., but in other ways I disagree for these reasons..., for example...***

Spot the Level

Read the following and state on which level the two answers are.

► *Sex before marriage is not always wrong; it depends on the circumstances.* Do you agree? Give reasons for your answer, showing that you have thought about more than one point of view. (5 marks)

Answer One In some ways I disagree with the statement. If you live in a society where people don't have sex before marriage, then it is unlikely you will. Peer pressure makes that too difficult. You might live in a Muslim country, and be a Muslim. In this case, not only is sex before marriage against your religion, it is also against the law, and could end in corporal punishment or imprisonment. The Qur'an gives both of these as the appropriate punishment, 'The fornicator should be flogged'.

On the other hand, I actually agree in some ways. It is quite common in the UK to have sex before marriage – you find out whether or not you are compatible in that area. Also the Church of England recognises that people will have sex before marriage, and speaks of sex in terms of the ultimate expression of love between two people in a permanent relationship – that doesn't mention marriage. What about people who are homosexual? They might be in a permanent relationship, which has lasted years and will last years more. They can't get married – it isn't an option for them, so sex before marriage has to be okay in that case.

Answer Two I disagree because some religions say it is wrong. Their holy book says so, and they must follow those rules. Rules are rules, really. You have to follow them, or they wouldn't be rules.

Go back to the questions set at the beginning of this Unit (p42). Answer them now, in the light of the work you have done on the Unit. Take each to be worth five marks. Use the Level of Response table opposite to help you.

What about the range of topics within the Unit. Can you answer these?

1 State two ways in which Christian parents might learn God's will.   (2 marks)

2 What responsibilities do husbands and wives take on in any one religious tradition?   (6 marks)

3 How might the parents of a follower be involved in the choice of marriage partner in any one religious tradition?   (2 marks)

4 Besides bringing up children, give two other purposes of marriage according to a religious tradition.   (4 marks)

5 Explain differing attitudes towards divorce in two religious traditions you have studied.   (8 marks)

6 State three reasons why a Christian would regard adultery as wrong.   (3 marks)

Did you find any of these questions difficult? Try these tips to help you gain maximum marks on each.

1 Ignore the word *parents*, you need to state two sources of authority, that's all.

2 Use the vows to help you – go through them, they are telling you what responsibilities a Christian couple take on. That is the easiest tradition to talk about. Explaining what each will mean in terms of married life will push you into the higher half of the available marks.

3 That's about arranged marriage, or parental approval.

4 Ignore the first half, just state two purposes of marriage.

5 The important word is *differing* – you must give two different attitudes. It's easiest to start with the Roman Catholic tradition – it is the only one to say divorce is always wrong.

6 Choose religious reasons as far as possible – this *is* an RE exam! Use everyday responses only when you run out of religious ones.

SIX

7 Prejudice and Discrimination

Prejudice is when a person has a preconceived idea about something; the idea is often unfavourable, and is not based on adequate facts. It is often a word used to describe a person's dislike of other people who are of a certain group, which could be to do with religion, race, age or appearance.

Discrimination is when a person is singled out because they are different in some way, and so are treated differently. This can be positive or negative discrimination, i.e. you can treat them better because of who or what they are, or worse for the same reason.

For this Unit, you have to

- understand both of these words

- know of some types of prejudice (at least two)

- know the attitudes of two religious traditions towards prejudice and discrimination in general, and to the two types you have studied in particular.

The attitude of the religious traditions is based on three concepts, for the purpose of this Unit. You will need to understand these concepts. When you answer questions on this Unit, try to keep these in mind, they will help to structure your response. The concepts are:

equality – that everyone is as important and valuable as each other

justice – that everyone is entitled to the same rights and treatment

community – that we are one community and should act as such.

► Looking at Prejudice and Discrimination

Think about the following questions – the pictures on the opposite page may help you.

► *What sorts of prejudice are there?*
Have you ever been the victim of prejudice? (How did you feel?)
Why are people prejudiced? Why are some people the victims of prejudice?
What can be done to fight prejudices, and change attitudes?

Challenging Prejudice

Everyone can be guilty of prejudice at times, though not everyone puts that into practice and becomes discriminatory.

Accepting that prejudice and discrimination are wrong, how could you challenge the prejudices illustrated below?

Prejudice is based on ignorance. We can have prejudices for many reasons. If the first three teachers you met when you first came to school were all really strict, even unfair, you might think that must be true of all the teachers in that school. It probably isn't, but those experiences have coloured your view. If I've only ever been told terrible things about people of a certain colour, I probably won't trust them easily when I actually meet them. My upbringing has taught me that. I might have seen something on TV that was itself very biased, and I believed it all, so I am biased. There are lots of reasons why I might be prejudiced.

It only takes someone to be (or be perceived to be) different in some way for them to be potentially a victim of prejudice. That difference marks people out – individually and in groups.

Prejudice is a terrible thing. It can destroy people's lives; it can end lives. Religious traditions all make strong statements against prejudice and discrimination. There is evidence within most religions of fighting prejudice and discrimination. In other words, followers of religious traditions put their beliefs into action by trying to live in ways which do not show prejudice, and by fighting prejudice itself.

The Basics

① Explain the words *prejudice* and *discrimination*.

② Why do some people hold prejudices?

③ What types of prejudice are there?

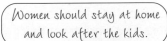
Women should stay at home and look after the kids.

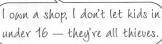
Two men holding hands — that's disgusting!

Nursing is a woman's job.

I own a shop, I don't let kids in under 16 — they're all thieves.

It's okay to pick on him, he's a swot!

Look at those fat people — eating must be their job and hobby!

We only have Asian lads in our football team.

seven

► Equality, Justice and Community

These are the three important concepts underpinning the religious attitudes to prejudice and discrimination. In your responses to exam questions, you should bear them in mind, and use them to give a structure to your work.

► *What does each word mean?*

► *Think about each word — how should it affect attitudes?*

Look at the table on the opposite page. Choose two religious traditions from it. Try to work out the attitude each would have concerning the three concepts.

You have seen that all religious traditions believe in the equality of humans, because God created all people equally. We should treat everyone as equals for the same reason, but also because that is how we would want to be treated (Judaism and Christianity). This equality demands that everyone should live in harmony and justice (Judaism, Islam, Christianity, Sikhism). The traditions even show examples of trying to promote that (Judaism, Sikhism). After all, we are all one nation or community (Christianity, Sikhism, Judaism) as we are God's creation. Even where differences of religious tradition occur, there is a sense of maintaining that tolerance and harmony (Judaism).

Definitions

Equality means having the same value and worth. In other words, no person is more important than any other.

Justice means fairness, that is, that everyone has the same rights, and should be treated in the same, fair manner.

Community is a label for a group of people – same area, same country, same religion, same species, even.

The Basics

① Choose two religious traditions. Using quotations from the table, and any others you know, outline the attitude of each tradition to the three concepts.

② In your opinion, following these concepts, how should each of the two traditions respond to issues of prejudice and discrimination?

Moving on ...

The exam requires you to be able to discuss two types of prejudice, and specific religious responses to them.

On the following pages are three types of prejudice – racism, sexism, and homophobia. The work from this page spread is general, but usually religious attitudes to the specific types of prejudice are themselves very specific. Use these topics to support the work on specific prejudices.

seven

	CHRISTIAN		MUSLIM		SIKH		JEWISH
1	*John 13 v 34 –* love one another.	1	All Muslims are equal. Muslim Declaration of Human Rights	1	*Adi Granth 557 –* Those who love God, love everybody.	1	*Leviticus 19 –* And if a stranger should live in your country, you must do him no wrong … love him as you love yourself.
2	*Acts 17 v 26 –* And He made from one every nation of men to live on all the face of the earth.	2	*Qur'an 3 v 104 –* Let there be a community among you who will invite others to do good, command what is proper and forbid what is improper.	2	*Mul Mantra –* This God is One … the Creator of all things.	2	The Seven Noachim Precepts are a set of rules for all men to live by. These include the promotion of justice.
3	*Galatians 3 v 28 –* There is neither Jew nor Greek, there is neither slave nor free, there is neither male nor female; for you are all one in Christ Jesus.	3	*Qur'an 4 v 58 –* Whenever you judge between people, you should judge with justice.	3	At a gurdwara, Sikhs hold the langar – community meal – after services. Everyone is welcome.	3	*Micah 6 v 8 –* He has showed you, O man, what is good; and what does God require of you but to do justice, love kindness, and walk humbly with your God?
4	*Matthew 7 v 12 –* so whatever you wish that men would do to you, do to them also.	4	*Qur'an 49 v 6 –* You who believe, if some scoundrel should bring you a piece of news, clear up the facts lest you hurt some folk out of ignorance.	4	*Adi Granth 349 –* Know people by the light which illuminates them, not by their caste.	4	As early as the 2nd century BCE, Jewish leaders were saying that Jews and non-Jews should live in harmony, helping and accepting each other.
5	*Genesis 1 v 27 –* So God created man in his own image, in the image of God. He created him; male and female He created them.	5	*Qur'an 60 v 8 –* Allah loves the fair-minded.	5	*Akal ustal 85 v 15* – To recognise the oneness of all humanity is an essential pillar of Sikhism … humanity world-wide is made up of one race.	5	*Genesis 12 v 2 –* I will make you into a great nation, and I will bless you. (Uses the Hebrew word *goy* which includes anyone of any religion in later Jewish writing.)
6	*Luke 10 v 30–37 –* In the Parable of the Good Samaritan, the man who was helped was helped because of his need, not because of who he was.	6	*Qur'an 3 v 103 –* Cling firmly together by means of Allah's rope, and do not be divided.	6	At a service, anyone can read the Guru Granth Sahib, or can lead the service.		

seven

▶ **Racism**

Legally and morally, racism and racist behaviour are unacceptable. Why should a person's skin colour, or their home country, count against them? The law believes that too. In Britain there are no laws that cover only white people. Racist behaviour can cost a person dearly – it is an accepted reason for exclusion from school, for example, or you can lose your job.

Definition

Racism is the belief that the colour of a person's skin, or their race, determines their ability. It is also the belief that some races are superior to others. Commonly, racist describes a person who discriminates negatively against those of a different race or skin colour.

'All human beings are born free and equal in dignity and rights ... should act towards one another in a spirit of brotherhood; that everyone is entitled to all the rights and freedom ... without distinction of any kind.'

Universal Declaration of Human Rights

The Christian View

Christians are united in their condemnation of racism. This is best expressed in *Galatians 3 v 28* 'There is neither Jew nor Greek ... you are all one in Christ Jesus.' You'll recognise this from p61, where there are other useful quotes. What are they? Essentially, Christianity claims we are all God's creation, and from one source. This makes us all the same, equal.

There are some Bible quotes which help specifically with the issue of racism. Check out the story of Jonah in the Old Testament. God punishes him for his refusal to go to the people of Ninevah. This racism is punished. Jesus helped anyone who needed help, and promoted this as an ideal. We see this in *Luke 7 v 1–10* (healing a Roman centurion's slave), and *Luke 10 v 25–36* (the Parable of the Good Samaritan). In fact, one of the main messages of the Gospel of Luke is that Jesus came for everyone – regardless

of race, status, religion. Find the quotes, make notes of their content and what they mean in terms of this issue.

Looking at Vatican II, we can see clearly the Roman Catholic attitude, which condemns racism totally:

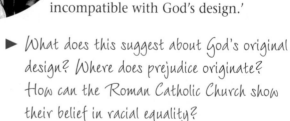

'Every form of social or cultural discrimination in fundamental personal rights on the grounds of sex, race, colour, social conditions, language or religion must be curbed and eradicated as incompatible with God's design.'

▶ *What does this suggest about God's original design? Where does prejudice originate? How can the Roman Catholic Church show their belief in racial equality?*

In 1985, the Church of England said that racism was still a challenge to be overcome. This was stated in a book called *Faith in the City* (CHP, 1985), and was a reflection of the General Synod in 1977. There it had been stated that the Church had a duty to stand up against anyone who tried to say some races were superior, and that each Church should do what it could locally to promote inter-racial harmony. The Church continues to do both.

▶ *How can churches practically fulfil these duties?*

The Muslim View

Islamic people have often been victims of prejudice. Their skin colour and their religion have given a focus to racism.

Islam considers all to be equal, all created by God. 'Among God's signs are the creation of the heavens and earth, and the variations in your languages and your colours.' *Qur'an 30 v 22*. 'Mankind! We created you from a single pair ... made you into nations and tribes, that you may know one another'. *Qur'an 49 v 13*.

Prophet Muhammad had non-Arabian friends and followers. When someone tried to make an issue out of their attendance to mosque, Muhammad was very angry, saying all were equal.

▶ *How does Islam explain the different races? What does this imply for racism? Following Prophet Muhammad's example, how should Muslims behave towards others?*

Islam calls the Muslim community the Umma. It covers people from all over the world, and is best seen in the hajj (pilgrimage), where all nations are represented. Anyone is welcome to become a Muslim – regardless of colour or race.

In the UK the Muslim community has set up *Muslims Against Racism*, which fights racism, and supports its victims.

▶ *Is it enough to not be racist? Do Muslims, for example, have a moral duty to be active in destroying racism also?*

The Jewish View

Much of Jewish history shows the Jews as victims of racism. The Jewish law and way of life can make the Jewish people stand out. This has given them a separate racial and cultural identity, as well as a different religion, and has resulted in discrimination. We call this *anti-semitism*.

At times, Jews have found it illegal to keep their faith; or to own a business; their rights have been denied; they have been forced to live in ghettos; anti-Jewish laws have been passed; and, they have been hounded and murdered. Perhaps of all faiths, the Jewish people know best what it is to be discriminated against.

Racism is wrong. *Leviticus* orders Jews to treat strangers (non-Jews) equally (p61). *Genesis 1 v 27* says all are made in God's image, and, later, that all nations came from a single man and woman (Adam and Eve). These are from the Torah – the word of God. *Leviticus* is law, binding on Jews.

▶ *Do you think that people such as the Jews would be more or less likely to be racist given their historical experience? Would they be more or less active in fighting racism?*

seven

Fighting Racism

Malcolm X

Theodore Herzl

All religious traditions consider racism wrong and believe it is right to stand up to it. You could look at the work of such Christians as Martin Luther King, Trevor Huddlestone, and Desmond Tutu. They were all outspoken in their condemnation of the racist societies in which they lived. They all fought non-violently to change society, and give equal rights to all people. For example, King organised strikes, demonstrations and rallies.

▶ *What non-violent methods are available to religious groups in Britain when fighting racism?*

The Islamic fight against racism can be seen through the work of *Muslims against Racism*. Again, their fight is non-violent. Organisations, such as the Muslim Educational Trust, publish books to help non-Muslims understand better the Muslims around them. Better understanding leads to more tolerance and harmony. Non-violence is also visible in the work of Malcolm X, and in the work of the Nation of Islam, such as the *Million Man* marches in the USA. However, Muslims are expected to hit back to defend themselves if attacked. 'Attack anyone who attacks you to the same extent as he attacked you.' *Qur'an 2 v 194*. This led to Malcolm X, amongst others, agreeing with violent ways of fighting racism in the USA.

Desmond Tutu

▶ *Which is more effective — violence or non-violence? In what ways? Is there a need for both?*

People such as Theodore Herzl (1850–1904) have fought to end discrimination of the Jewish people. Herzl's work was all through discussion and meeting – non-violent. He wrote pamphlets to try to educate people and bring understanding, as well as calling for a Jewish state (which now exists in the form of Israel). The Holocaust memorial of Yad Vashem, in Israel, is a testimony to the fight against discrimination. Part of it remembers the efforts made by non-Jews to help the Jews. Jewish people point to the past to learn for the future.

The Basics

Choose two religious traditions. What is the attitude of each to racism? Make sure you include the teachings to support the points you make.

How might members of each of the two religious traditions respond to examples of racism?

Specifically, how could a member of each tradition respond to the following examples of racism?
(a) a pupil in school who is the victim of an incident of racial abuse
(b) a group of pupils who are always racist in their behaviour towards others in the school
(c) a racist group organising a march through their hometown
(d) racist chanting on the terraces of a football club, which happens regularly

seven

► Sexism

Definition

Sexism is prejudice or discrimination against people, especially women, because of their sex.

This issue deals with how right it is to treat people differently because of their sex, but also brings in the question of whether different treatment also means inequality.

Are men and women equal? Give some examples which show they are. Give some examples which show they are not.

Does society make people feel equal or unequal? Is it possible for people to be told they aren't equal, so they begin to feel that way? Or do you automatically recognise it happening to you? Does one person have the right to look at someone else's life and make judgements about equality, or how they should feel?

We've already seen that religions view all people as equal, all created by God. When we get down to the level of male and female, does that teaching ring true? Have you seen as many women as men priests? Do women get to make as many decisions as men? Do women get to make the *big* decisions at all?

What about the idea of men and women being equal, but different? What could you say to support that idea? Or to dismiss it?

So, Are Men and Women Equal?

There has been a debate within the Church of England in recent years about this through the issue of ordination. Up until the late 1980s, all vicars were male. Women were not allowed to hold this position of responsibility within the Church. At a Synod, that position was changed. Women were accepted to be ordained. Once again, the Church of England showed a willingness to change in response to a changing society. A number of vicars left the Church of England, showing their disapproval, as did some of the congregation. In 1994, the Pope wrote an apostolic letter stating that women could not become priests – it was inappropriate and broke with tradition. In fact, the rule was said to be part of the *deposit of faith* – truths handed down by Jesus himself.

Why the Big Argument?

Traditionally, going back to Jesus, there have been no female Church leaders. It is wrong to break with tradition, which clearly comes from God.

Jesus had only male disciples. He spoke to women, even taught them, but he himself gave them no power or authority. They can listen and help, but they cannot lead.

During each month, women menstruate. They are not then fit to give communion rites.

Jesus' message was for all. In the early Church, women such as Priscilla were important church leaders. Her husband, who worked with her, never felt threatened.

Tradition is based in the times it came from. In the past societies have been male dominated, so women could not have such authority. Times have changed. We should try to reflect the current time.

Sometimes, it is impossible for a man to understand. Women are much better listeners and have much more patience. A big part of the job of a vicar is counselling and support and women are much better at this. For example, how can we expect woman to visit a male priest for counselling and support if she has been raped?

Pick out the arguments put forward by the two vicars. How strong are these arguments?

Equal ... but Different?

So, what of this argument? Men and women are clearly different. Are there any roles which only men, or only women, can fulfil?

Islam states in the the Qur'an and Hadith the importance of women. Prophet Muhammad, in his farewell speech, said

'Women have certain rights over you, and you have certain rights over them. Treat them well, and be kind to them, for they are your partners and committed helpers.' When asked who deserved the best care, he replied 'Your mother, your mother, your mother, then your father and then your nearest relatives.' Women go on hajj, they follow all the same rules as male Muslims and they believe they can go to heaven (just as Muslim men can).

Islam does split the roles of men and women up, and gives each duties, which it considers equal and complementary. Both sexes should follow the faith; should dress modestly; should be faithful. Women have responsibility for bringing up young children and girls, and are in charge of the house; men have responsibility for earning money for what the family needs, and for the religious education of boys. Both should comfort and help the other.

► *Are these equally important roles? Are they equal roles?*

In the West, people often think of Islam as a male-dominated religion, where women have few, if any, rights. Consider Afghanistan, for example, where many women who worked were dragged from offices and executed when Taliban Muslims took Kabul. However, it is true that when Islam began, women were given rights in law, which were far advanced for the time. Women were suddenly allowed to inherit, dowries were banned, female infanticide was made illegal. We must also not forget that in Islamic countries, there is little discussion of inequality. Most women do not even consider it. They live in a culture where this way of life is the norm.

► *Why do you think that is? Are Westerners imposing their own feelings, and trying to tell Muslim women how they should feel? Would Muslim women in Britain, for example, view their counterparts in Islamic countries in terms of equality?*

The Basics

① Define *sexism*. Give some examples of positive and negative sexist discrimination.

② Choose two religious traditions. For each explain the attitude of the tradition to sexual equality.

③ For the same traditions, explain their attitude to women.

④ Inequality is not being given a choice. No one can say I have no equality if I choose to live in a particular way, with other options available, e.g. stay at home and look after my family. Discuss this idea.

⑤ Discrimination comes from people's interpretation of a religion, not the religion itself. When men start a religion, you get sexism. Do you agree? Explain your answer.

seven

► Homophobia

As late as the beginning of the 21st century, the age of consent for lesbians was not stated. It was age 18 for gay men and 16 for heterosexuals. Gay rights groups campaign to change this, so that the age of consent for any sexual encounter is the same. They believe that to have different age limits is a form of discrimination. Those who disagree with the change believe that young men should be protected from older homosexuals who may take advantage of their emotions. They feel that people do not know they are homosexual until later in life. Many just feel homosexuality is wrong and unnatural, so such people should be given no rights.

► *Is this discrimination? Why do you think society has changed over the last hundred years to gradually be more accepting of gay men and lesbians?*

Gay and lesbian people can face much hostility. Prejudice is displayed in many of the same ways, whatever its type. In some ways though, the hostility the gay community faces is different from that faced by other groups, because it often involves rejection (and worse) by their own families. It is the most recently acknowledged, and condemned, form of prejudice, and these people are not protected as specifically as other groups. For example, the assault of a gay man is *assault* in police records, whilst that of a person of colour is additionally labelled *racist*.

► *Why do you think this group is the last to receive specific protection in law, and society's morals?*

The Muslim View

Homosexuality is condemned in Islamic law. It is considered unnatural and against God. Homosexual acts are punishable under Islamic law – by imprisonment or death. Part of the reason is that no pregnancy can result, part because the family is considered to be the fundamental building block of society, and same sex couples are not seen as families. The Qur'an says that if two people of the same gender have sex, but are sorry, they should be left alone. However, if they repeat the act, so are obviously not sorry, they should be punished. This isn't about prejudice and discrimination, it is about law and order, as far as Islam is concerned.

The Christian View

The Roman Catholic view is quite unequivocal – homosexuality is wrong when acted upon. That is, the Roman Catholic Church believes that some people cannot help having homosexual feelings; however, it is wrong to take part in homosexual acts, and we have the freedom of will to choose not to. Two people of the same sex can't have a child together, and since sex is for procreation, same sex acts are wrong. It is unnatural. Having condemned homosexual acts, the Church also condemns any discrimination against homosexuals.

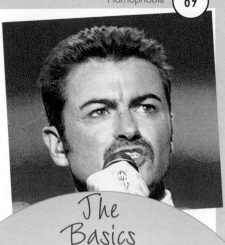

► *What should the Church do if it has gay parishioners who are the victims of prejudice?*

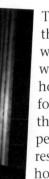

The Church of England in 1987 said that homosexual genital acts were not what God had intended, and so were wrong. Those who were active homosexuals should seek forgiveness for their actions. However, it also said that sex was acceptable within permanent loving relationships. As a result, some vicars will welcome homosexuals, whilst others stand by the same view put forward by the Catholic Church. In 1991, it re-emphasised the need to speak out against homophobia, and to protect victims of it.

► *Do you think prejudice and discrimination are encouraged by classing something as wrong or unnatural? Try to give some examples to demonstrate your points.*

The Basics

① Define *homophobia*. Give examples of it.

② Why do you think people might be homophobic?

③ Choose two religious traditions. Explain their attitude to homophobic prejudice and discrimination. Use the information from this page, and from p68 to construct your answers.

④ As long as the religions call gay sex unnatural, people will have an excuse to victimise other human beings. How far do you agree? Give reasons and explain your answer.

Acceptance?

It sounds as if religions just see same sex relationships as wrong. Do they?

The Metropolitan Community Church is a Protestant Church, which welcomes homosexuals. The Quaker Lesbian and Gay Fellowship does too. Both claim that God created us all equally, and we are all special. God loves us all, whatever our sexuality. Jesus said, 'Whosoever believes in me shall have everlasting life' – he didn't make any exceptions. He also helped and welcomed outcasts and any others society tried to reject.

The Methodist Church has said that no practising homosexual or lesbian should be rejected for training for ordination on the grounds of the expression of their sexuality alone. Homosexuals can serve God as ministers.

◄◄ Check out attitudes to sex in Unit 6 pp 46–47, and to sacredness of life in Unit 9 p81.

seven

Exam Tips

According to the course specification, you need to know: why people are prejudiced; two forms of prejudice; and, what religious attitudes are to prejudice, especially in relation to the concepts of justice, equality and community. Do you know these?

Try these questions. There are some tips on answering each. Use this book, or your notes, to help you.

1   *Choose two different religious traditions and outline the teaching of each about prejudice and discrimination.*   (9 marks)

State the traditions, use quotations, explain the teachings. Use at least two quotes or teachings for each tradition.

2   *How do people in one religious tradition apply their beliefs about prejudice and discrimination in practical ways?*   (6 marks)

In other words, what can people do to fight prejudice and discrimination, since they all disagree with it? Think up ways an individual could act, how a group could act, what a Church could do. Think about behaviour, speech, attitudes. Think positively (e.g. welcome people), as well as aggressively (e.g. demonstrate). Remember, this GCSE is 'religious' so make sure you have at least some religious elements in it.

3   *By sending their children to religious schools, some religious believers are encouraging them to be prejudiced against others.* Do you agree? Give reasons, showing you have thought about more than one point of view.

(5 marks)

Remember – two sides to be argued. Give reasons and examples.

Time Test

Here's another set of questions. Give yourself 25 minutes – no books.

1   Explain, using examples, the difference between prejudice and discrimination.

(4 marks)

2   What teaching is given about prejudice and discrimination in the sacred texts of one religious tradition?   (5 marks)

3   Describe how the teachings you have outlined in Question 2 are put into practice in this tradition with regard to (a) people of different races and (b) women.   (6 marks)

4   *An Anglican bishop has argued that it is not always wrong to discriminate against other people; it depends on the circumstances.* Do you agree with his view? Give reasons for your opinion, showing that you have thought about more than one point of view.   (5 marks)

Evaluative Questions

These questions often prove difficult. You read something, and agree or disagree. The question then asks you whether you agree or disagree. It insists you talk about a number of viewpoints. How can you do that if you only either agree or disagree? Sorry, you are going to have to learn! Try taking these sorts of questions, and writing them as a dialogue between two or more imaginary people. That way, you start to build up discussions of a statement. Use p66 as an example.

The final exam lasts 1 hour and 45 minutes. It totals 80 marks (4 questions each of 20 marks). That is an average of 1¼ minutes per mark. Use that to help you pace yourself in the exam, so for a question worth 6 marks, you should be taking no more than 7½ minutes.

8 World Poverty

What do these words mean to you?   **Wealth**   **Poverty**

▶ *Where does poverty exist? Think of some examples.*

It will be helpful to you in this Unit to collect newspaper and other articles about poverty, and work in the field of poverty. This will give you real examples to use in the exam.

Look at these statements. Can you comment on them?

① There'll always be poor people, we can't help all of them.

② They are poor because they are lazy.

③ You shouldn't give money to homeless people. They should get a job, and anyway they chose to sleep on the streets.

④ Poverty is almost always because of what humans have done, or chosen not to do. Governments keep people poor, whilst nature makes it even worse.

⑤ Why don't they use proper equipment like tractors – then they'd have more food.

⑥ Even when they have a famine, countries still send food to rich countries to pay their debts.

⑦ We are one global family, we need to support our brothers and sisters wherever they are.

The key concepts in this Unit are

• stewardship (responsibility for looking after something, in this case, others in the world),

• justice (fairness for all),

• community (the idea of people being one community which should help everyone within it, or different communities supporting each other).

Use these concepts when trying to answer questions.

Surfing

Lots of the topics in this course can be checked out on the Internet. Make use of this very valuable tool, if you can. For example, on this topic, you need to be able to discuss the work of one religious organisation. Try these websites. www.cafod.org; www.christian-aid.org.uk; www.islamic-relief.org.uk.

Definitions

Wealth is to have a large amount of money and/or valuable material possessions.

Poverty is the condition of being without adequate food, money, shelter, or a lack of the elements conducive to these.

► Exploring Poverty

The UN and World Health Organisation have identified six basic needs. These are broken down into the things we cannot live without, and the things that allow us to obtain the necessities. They are food, water, shelter, employment, education and healthcare. Each requirement has to be adequate; for example, you might have access to healthcare, but it is of a very poor standard.

► *Why is each of these important? How could the lack of any cause hardship? Think about Britain, considering these elements, is there poverty in Britain?*

Some Facts

● At least one in eight people in the world has inadequate food.

● Tens of millions of people die each year because of dirty water, which itself causes over three-quarters of all sickness and disease.

● Nearly three-quarters of people in developing countries can only get minimal healthcare at best.

● Only two adults in five can read and write. Only one in four children in developing countries has any education beyond primary level.

● Hundreds of millions of people in developing countries have no job, most living off what they can grow.

● Homes in developing countries are frequently cramped, electricity is a luxury, and running water non-existent.

How Help is Given

We can split the work of organisations and individuals into three broad areas. Most deal in all three.

Firstly, fund-raising work. For an organisation to be able to do anything, it has to have money. Raising money is done in all kinds of ways, both large and small scale.

► *Can you think of ways in which money can be raised?*

Secondly, organisations campaign to get change. Most developing countries need the support of foreign governments, e.g. through cancelling debt.

► *What methods could be used to make a representation to a government, or to b[ ] to get change?*

Thirdly, organisations try to educate pe[ ] especially the young, so that they will [ ] to help or to force change. Young people are part of the future, they need to understand the situation and how they can change it. If they learn new attitudes, they can make a difference in the future.

► *How could organisations educate people — what resources could they create, or forms of media could they use? Is there a difference between educating adults, and educating children?*

► *Do you think that religious organisations could try to do anything else to bring help to developing countries?*

Direct Help

Organisations split the direct work into two areas – relief and aid. Relief is help given in times of disaster, or absolute need, e.g. in an earthquake-stricken area. Aid is help given to effect a change, and improve a situation for the future, e.g. setting up a well-building project, or setting up a project to train *barefoot* doctors.

Tough Decisions

Imagine you lead an aid agency. How would you respond to the following requests? What support would you give? How could you publicise and raise money? Try to be realistic – work out the priorities for each situation and decide what any agency could reasonably be expected to do.

Our country has suffered an earthquake. Sixty per cent of the people are displaced, and now have no homes. Many people have disappeared — we think they are buried. The people are frightened another earthquake will happen, but want to help to find their loved ones. Our capital city was devastated, and many communication links are damaged.

Our village is a shanty village outside Sao Paolo. We have lost many of our young people because of dirty water. Our houses are cramped and we have no electricity. We get water from the town, but it is a trek.

My country is torn by civil war. It is terrible — family fights family, no one is spared. Thanks to the fighting, our food supplies are affected — not enough people work in the fields. Our hospitals are damaged by the fighting, and many doctors and nurses are dead. Medicines are few. Many people are homeless. The UN has set up some refugee camps, but these are in need of supplies and workers.

My country is very poor. The levels of healthcare and education are both low. We want to advance as a nation, and compete in the world. Many of my people do work and their produce is sold to dealers in other countries. They earn very little for this, but haven't the business knowledge to improve their lot.

The Basics

①
What are the basic needs of humans?

②
What can you say about people in situations of poverty regarding these needs?

③
How do organisations divide their help?

④
What is done in terms of direct help? Give examples of these.

⑤
It is a waste of time spending money on people in other countries. There is too much to be done in our own.
How far do you agree? Give reasons and explain your answer.

⑥
A church which really cares about the poor, can never itself be a rich church. How far do you agree? Give reasons and explain your answer.

► The Christian Attitude to Poverty

Why Christians Help

Read the following comments about helping others. Use them to create a set of guidelines about why Christians help other people.

Jesus helped many people, regardless of race, wealth, status. Christians are told to follow Jesus' example as a demonstration of their faith.

In the Parable of the Rich Fool (*Luke 12 v 16–21*), the rich man's harvest is too vast for his barns. Instead of sharing his good fortune, he has new, bigger barns built. God decides that he will die that night. He will be unable to enjoy this wealth.

In *Acts 4 v 32–35*, the early Christian community is encouraged to share all they have, as if everything belonged to them collectively. It is then reissued to people according to their need.

In the Story of the Final Judgement (*Matthew 25 v 31–46*), the sheep and goats are split up at Judgement Day. The sheep are sent to heaven, because they helped whoever needed help. The goats are denied heaven because they did not think of anyone but themselves. Helping others is likened to helping God.

1 John 3 v 17–18. If a rich person sees his brother in need, yet closes his heart to him, how can he claim that he loves God? My children, our love should not be just words and talk; it must be true love which shows itself in action.

Luke 14 v 13–14 But when you give a banquet, invite the poor, the lame, the blind, and you will be blessed, because they cannot repay you. You will be repaid at the resurrection of the just.

The Parable of the Good Samaritan (*Luke 10 v 30–37*) answers the question of 'Who is my neighbour?' It tells us that whoever needs help is the one we should help.

Genesis 1 v 27 So God created man in his own image ... male and female he created them.

The Basics

Use information from this double page to answer these.

① Why should Christians help others? Use quotations to strengthen the points you make.

② Describe the work of one Christian organisation. Use quotes to show how it is fulfilling Christian motivation.

③ How do you think religions should decide who they help?

In your guidelines, are there any barriers to helping people? Any particular people excluded, or included? What can you say about equality, justice and community (our three concepts)? How do these affect how Christians act?

Christian Organisations

Christian Aid
Set up 1964

Christian ♦ Aid
We believe in life before death

History replaced an organisation, which had helped refugees. The work of Christian Aid has developed from refugee work, to disaster relief work, to aid projects, to development education and campaigning for a fairer world. Now involved in all these areas at the same time.

Examples of projects helped emergency grants for the homeless in El Salvador after the earthquake in 2001; AIDS project in Jamaica to provide medical care, support and education; work in Brazil to increase people's rights, e.g. farmers receiving a fair price for their crops.

CAFOD
The Catholic Fund for Overseas Development
Set up 1962

History historically, Catholic Churches generated charity funds on one specific day of each year.

They themselves decided what to do with this money. CAFOD was the organisation set up to centralise this fund-raising, and be more effective and wide-ranging with it. Work which began as disaster relief and aid work, now includes campaigning for a fairer world, and a vast array of educational work, including a schools magazine, as well as Church magazines.

An example of a project helped funding water pipes for a Brazilian shanty town to give access to clean water (this project gave the people belief in themselves and their ability to change their lives, as well as helping with health problems directly).

Both organisations are Christian, and the bulk of their work is with overseas clients. They respond to disasters by sending at least supplies, but often volunteers, to help. For example, in the recent Salvadoran earthquake, both sent medicines, food and blankets. Perhaps more important is their aid work. They use similar methods to decide who should get help.

► *Why do you think they don't help everyone who asks?*

Firstly, some representation is made by, or on behalf of, the needy communities, to explain what they feel they need. This is considered both in theory, and at the actual place.

► *Why do you think they send people to check out these requests?*

If it is approved, then money or people are sent. Often communities do the work themselves, and go on to do more things as well – this becomes a start for a better future.

► *Why should they be encouraged to help themselves?*

The money raised comes from many sources – charity shops, collections, donations, bequests, sponsored events and sponsorships.

Both organisations feel it is important that young people, especially, know about their work. Young people are the donors of the future, they are also the people who can make changes.

► *Why should people be more likely to help if they know about the problems?*

► The Muslim Attitude to Poverty

Why Muslims Help Others

Read the following comments about helping others. Use them to create a set of guidelines about why Muslims help other people.

You are miserly at the expense of your own soul. (Hadith and Qur'an)

Islam preaches the equality and brotherhood of all people. The worldwide Islamic community is the Umma. People who become Muslims from another faith are called *reverts* because it is believed everyone is born a Muslim.

He who eats and drinks whilst his brother goes hungry is not one of us. (Hadith)

For the love of Allah, give from your wealth to your relatives, to orphans, to the needy, to the traveller, to those who ask, and to release the slave. (Qur'an)

Talking about those who store up money and possessions in this lifetime, the Qur'an says; Their works are fruitless in this world and in the hereafter, and they will lose all spiritual good.

May Allah accept the work we have done for his sake. (Muslim prayer)

Everyday two angels come down from heaven; one says *Allah, Compensate everyone who gives in your name*; the other says *Allah, Destroy every miser.*

The Basics

Use the information from this double page to help you answer these questions.

Outline the Muslim attitude to helping others. Use quotations to help support the points you make.

Describe the work of a Muslim organisation. Use quotes to show how they are fulfilling Muslim motivation.

Given that Islam believes all people were born Muslim, how can a Muslim religious organisation justify focusing its work on Islamic communities?

In your guidelines, are there any barriers to helping people? Any particular people excluded, or included? What can you say about equality, justice and community (our three concepts)? How do these affect how Muslims act?

Zakat

Accept zakat from their wealth; you will cleanse and purify them by means of it. *(Qur'an 9 v 103)*

It is a duty for all Muslims to pay zakat once each year (one of the Five Pillars). This is a sum of money – 2.5 per cent of all money accumulated in the year and is paid annually.

Zakat is meant only for the poor, the needy, those working at it, those whose hearts are being reconciled, for freeing captives and debtors, and for the traveller, as a duty imposed by God. *(Qur'an 9 v 60)*

This tells you who receives the money collected – clearly it should be used in part for charity work. So it is a Muslim's duty to help the poor.

▶ If it is a duty to pay zakat, should we expect to see Muslims living in poverty?

Sadaqah

This literally means charity. Muslims *must* give zakat, but they are encouraged to also give sadaqah. Everything about this is up to the person giving it – how much, when it is given, who it goes to. It doesn't have to be money either, it can be goods, time, advice – anything which will help. Allah rewards those who give sadaqah, he punishes those who don't give zakat – it's an important difference. Many Muslim families will pay to have an animal sacrificed on important occasions, to feed the poor, their neighbours and relatives. At hajj, the sacrifices are *Qurbani*, and the meat is distributed to the poor, as either tinned, preserved or fresh meat.

▶ Why should sadaqah carry more reward and praise than zakat?

▶ Find out about the different organisations you have met on the pages of this unit. Compare and contrast the work they do, and their motivation for doing that work.

Islamic Relief Worldwide

Set up   1984 in Europe.

History   the first Muslim Relief Agency in Europe, now provides humanitarian aid during emergency situations, and works for the long-term development of the world's poorest nations. It aims to try to alleviate the suffering of the needy wherever they are. The bulk of its development work is in Muslim countries.

Examples of projects helped
One of the first agencies to send help to Bosnia, Albania and Chechnya. The *Ramadan Package* in thirty countries, including Pakistan and Kashmir gave food parcels to the poor and needy. A free hospital and dispensary has been set up in Kashmir, whilst mobile health clinics are funded in Ingushetia.

► The Jewish Attitude to Poverty

Why Judaism Helps Others

Read the following comments about helping others. Use them to create a set of guidelines about why Jews help other people.

Poor people will always exist, so I command you. Open your hand to your brother, to the poor and needy in your land. *(Deuteronomy 15 v 9–11)*

Blessed is he who considers the poor. *(Psalms 41 v 1)*

Love the stranger, for you were strangers in Egypt. *(Deuteronomy 10 v 19)*

Charity is a matter of legal rightness in Judaism, expected of all men to all men.

We must support the poor among the Gentiles, even as we support the poor of Israel ... all in the interests of peace. *(Talmud)*

In *Leviticus 19*, we are told that there are legally assigned gifts for the poor. For example, from the harvest, any fallen crops, any field corners, any crops which grow in a fallow year, plus a tithe each year are for the poor.

Judaism believes we do not own our wealth, we are guardians of it for God. We should use it wisely.

Whom God loves, to him does he send a golden opportunity for charity.

In your guidelines, are there any barriers to helping people – any particular people excluded, or included? What can you say about equality, justice and community (our three concepts)? How do these affect how Jews act?

The Basics

①
Outline the Jewish attitude to helping those in need. Use quotes and examples to strengthen the points you make.

②
Outline the work of one Jewish organisation that works with the poor and needy. Show how this work fulfils Jewish motivation for helping.

③
Compare the two religious traditions you have studied. Is there a difference between their motivation for helping the poor? Do you think there would be a difference in the amount of help they give, either voluntarily, or through duty or law? Explain yourself.

④
Religious people are far more likely to help others – it's in their nature. How far do you agree? Give reasons and explain your answer.

Tzedekah

This word actually means righteousness, though it is the universal word for charity. Tzedekah is a commandment, a duty on all Jews, and it is more than money – it is about giving time and goods. Maimonides said that all men should give charity – even those receiving it. Everyone should donate a portion of what they receive – you could see this as the tithe which most Jews pay (five to ten per cent of income). Jewish people are encouraged to be charitable whenever they can, and synagogues are central to charity work.

Judaism does recognise that charity cannot be endless, and can be refused if it is a source of embarrassment to the receiver. Traditionally, Jews have been encouraged to loan money, or help people to set up in business as acts of charity. This enables someone to become self-sufficient, and also takes away the stigma of having needed charity.

► How could it be said that helping people become self-sufficient is a better use of charity?

Maimonides said 'The quality of mercy is characteristic of the Jewish people. They are like brothers … and if a brother shows no mercy towards a brother, who will?'

► How does the work of WJR show this attitude?

World Jewish Relief

Set up 1960s

History focused until 1996 on work with Jewish refugees all over the world, under the aim of supporting Jews in distress. Much of its work involves empowering local communities, i.e. teaching them to be self-sufficient. This enables WJR to move on and help other communities. Its work is now focused in the states which made up the Soviet Union, e.g. Ukraine. Additionally, it continues to give advice and support to any Jew needing such. In the main, its funding comes from the Jewish community.

Project outline

since the break-up of the Soviet Union, many elderly Jews and orphans have been left behind, unsupported. Their living conditions, based on their state pensions, do not cover normal costs of basic living. WJR supports many through food parcels and medical care. WJR runs orphanages in the Ukraine, which take in street children.

Exam Tips

For this topic, don't forget wealth and poverty are *relative*; there are wealthy people in every country, and poverty exists everywhere. This means that your answers to open questions can take into account the homeless person in Manchester, or the single mum who lives in a damp, one-bedroomed flat in London, or the family who cannot feed their children adequately from their farm in India. Don't just focus on the idea of *poor countries*.

With a partner, answer these questions orally.

① What is *compassion*?

② How can we benefit if we give to the poor?

③ Should we look after people in our own countries, before we look after those overseas? Explain.

④ How could a person help people in need?

Take it in turns to answer these questions.

① Choose any religious tradition. Take it in turns to give a reason why that religious tradition helps others. Gain one point for each agreed reason. Gain two points if you can think of a quote.

② Choose another religious tradition. Do the same.

③ Each choose a religious organisation. On paper jot down the following details – when it began, who it helps, how it raises money and examples of projects. See who can remember the most. Can you remember any missing details for your partner?

This topic commonly asks two main questions when it is part of the exam paper. Let's look at these and unpack them.

▶ *Outline the teachings of one/two religious tradition(s) about the use of wealth.*

This would be worth 4 marks, if one tradition, or 8, if two. You will need to make two or more points (for each), and explain them to get the full marks. We can rewrite the question as *why do … help others?* Let's take Islam – why do Muslims help others?

> *Muslims have a religious duty to help others. [They must pay zakat once each year, and part of this goes to charity, so they have an obligation to help the poor.]*

> *In the Qur'an, it says that Muslims should give from their wealth to lots of people including orphans and the needy. [To do this gains the love of Allah, and will benefit them on Judgement Day.]*

Try to think of two more reasons, make sure you give reasons and explanations.

▶ *Describe the work of one religious organisation, which helps the poor.*

This would usually be worth 4 marks. It *must* be a religious organisation.

To give a list of details may get you three of the four marks, but really you have to put it into a coherent block. A Level 4 answer (four marks) should contain specific information about who is helped, what help is given, and how the organisation raises the funds to do this, as well as awareness of the need.

Answer – CAFOD is the Catholic Fund for Overseas Development. It raises funds through collections in churches, sponsorships and donations generally. It tries to educate people which will encourage them to give more, e.g. through school and church CAFOD magazines. Its work supports people in deprived situations, for example, helping poor townships to create and build water supply systems, or medical centres. It also responds to emergency disaster situations, for example, it sent aid to the Salvadoran earthquake of 2001.

Try to do this for a different religious tradition.

9 War and Peace

The key concepts in this Unit are Peace, Justice and Sanctity of Life. You have met all of these before in other contexts. Look back through your notes to pick up some ideas useful to this topic.

Peace is obviously the absence of war. Can you describe peace? Is it more than no war?

Justice is the sense of fairness being applied.

Can we fight in a just way? Even if we set rules, can they ever be carried out perfectly (if at all)?

Sanctity of life is the idea that life is special or sacred. What message does that send to anyone thinking of fighting? If a government is religious, and holds to that concept, can they ever fight?

Let's look at war. Why do wars begin?

Imagine you are the leader of a country. With a partner, decide which of the following cases would lead you to declare war.

① Country X, with whom you have a treaty, has been invaded by Country Y.

② Country D, which used to be part of your Empire, is overthrown by a military coup. Do you declare war to put the original leaders back into power (who you had put into power in the first place)?

③ Country F successfully invades your country.

④ Country S unsuccessfully tries to invade your country.

⑤ Country B may have developed nuclear weapon capability. They are not friends of your own country.

⑥ Country V is massacring a group of its own people. There is huge uproar in your own country about this.

⑦ Country Q has outlawed a religion (which happens to be that of your own country). It is forcing all members of that religion either to leave (penniless), to convert to its own religion, or be executed.

⑧ Country N takes on a political ideology with which you do not agree, and which will harm your substantial trade links with it, as well as possibly in its area.

In each case, why did you decide to declare war, or not to? What might be the consequences of your decisions? Are there any totally acceptable reasons for war, or totally unacceptable ones?

For each case, if you did go to war, when would the war be ended? How would you make sure that your conditions of peace were kept?

► **Fighting a War**

The concept of justice is very important here. Have you ever thought about war? Can there be justice in war, when war is essentially about killing your opposite number?

There are rules of warfare, called the Geneva Conventions. These have been signed in part or in whole by most countries in the world. When you hear about war crimes trials, as happened in the recent Bosnian war, the people on trial have broken rules set within the Geneva Conventions.

Why do you think rules have been set for fighting wars? Do they work? Find out about the Geneva Conventions.

Imagine you are part of a team, which will create a set of rules for warfare. Here are some elements to consider, which may be additional to anything you come up with.

Captured prisoners

Field hospitals

Wounded soldiers (captured or on battlefield)

Enemy civilians

Legitimate targets

Extent of battlefield

Legitimate weapons

Thinking about Treatment of Prisoners

In terms of treatment, which of the following are acceptable or unacceptable, and why? Do you treat civilians in a different way from how you treat soldiers? Why?

Use of torture for punishment	Discrimination by religion
Use of torture for information	Discrimination by nationality
Use of hostage-taking	Discrimination by politics
Mass execution	Political indoctrination
Reprisal punishment/execution	Human shield tactics
Deportation	Rape and/or pillage
Discrimination by sex	Use of threats to obtain people, information etc.

► *If you didn't accept any of these, you already agree with the Geneva Conventions without even looking. How do you think these people should be treated whilst under your control in a war situation?*

► *Do you think that religious people would agree with the rules and guidelines you have created for war (given their ideas of justice, sanctity of life and peace)?*

► **Types of Weapons**

What are the types of weapons available to armies in modern warfare? How do you think weapons have changed over the last two centuries? What impact has this had?

There are four major categories of weapons.

Firstly, *conventional weapons*. These are weapons such as guns, knives, planes, ships, tanks that have  ordinary ammunition and impact. Most armed forces work with conventional weapons. They are allowed by the Geneva Conventions. These weapons are controllable or manageable in terms of their target.

► Is it always acceptable to use these weapons, considering that they do have specific targets?

Secondly, *nuclear weapons*. These are weapons of mass destruction which kill immediately, and their potential to destroy is long lasting, even after they have exploded. Their effect cannot be controlled in any clear way. There has never been a nuclear war, and it is believed that should one begin, the world would be destroyed.

► Why do you think countries have, but don't use, such weapons?

Thirdly, *chemical weapons*. These are weapons which have as their warhead a device containing chemicals, e.g. the bombs which released mustard gas during World War I, or the  napalm bombs, which the US army dropped on Vietnam; the napalm sticks to the skin, but it burns as it does so. They cannot be controlled very well. These are not acceptable under the Geneva Conventions.

► Why might these weapons be uncontrollable? Is it right that someone should suffer because of these weapons long after the war has ended? e.g. Agent Orange was dropped on Vietnamese forests in the 1960s to cause the leaves to drop, people were dusted with it, and even now suffer strange cancers.

Fourthly, *biological warfare*. This involves weapons, which release biological agents, such as viruses, when they are exploded. The contents can often be carried by the wind across great distances. Their aim is to kill or disable people via illness. They are not acceptable under the Geneva Conventions.

► Could there ever be any just use of such weapons?

nine

► The Christian Attitude to War and Peace

Jesus and Pacifism

Jesus only demonstrated peace in his teachings and behaviour.

In what ways can we see pacifism in these examples from the Bible?

> *Matthew 26 v 47–52* tells the story of Jesus' arrest. Jesus stopped his disciples from fighting, and went peacefully with his captors.
>
> 'Blessed are the peacemakers, for they shall be called the sons of God.' *(Matthew 5 v 9)*
>
> 'You have been taught: An eye for an eye. But I tell you this … If someone slaps you on the right cheek, turn and offer him your left.' *(Matthew 5 v 38–39)*
>
> 'You have heard it said: Love your friends, hate your enemies. But now I tell you: love your enemies, and pray for those who persecute you.' *(Matthew 5 v 43–44)*

The message of Christianity from its earliest days was one of peace, based on the above. Even today, that is the ideal. The Church of England in Synods that spanned the World Wars of the 20th century said, 'War as a method of settling international disputes is incompatible with the teaching and example of Jesus.' (Does that leave a gap for wars for other reasons?) Pope John Paul II, speaking in Coventry in 1982: 'All people must deliberately and resolutely commit themselves to the pursuit of peace.'

The Quakers (Society of Friends)

This group within Christianity is strongly pacifist. They follow this teaching from St Paul: 'Live in harmony with one another … If possible, so far as it depends on you, live peaceably with all … Never take revenge, leave it to God's anger … If your enemy is hungry, feed him … Do not be overcome by evil, but overcome evil with good.' *(Romans 12 v 16–21)*

Since Quakers emphasise that all relationships should be loving, their beliefs must exclude war. They have made stands against war throughout history, including demonstrating peacefully to make their point. Quakers do not join the armed forces, remaining conscientious objectors. They believe that discussion, mediation and reconciliation are the keys to solving difficulties, not fighting. That doesn't mean that they do not help out in times of war. Many Quakers try to lessen the effects of war, aiding in relief work or acting as medics. In times of peace, many Quakers are actively involved in trying to prevent war.

For Quakers, there is no just reason for war – 'We utterly deny all outward wars and strife and fighting with outward weapons, for any end or under any pretence whatsoever.'

► Look back to p81 and the list of wars. How might Quakers sort out these issues peacefully?

► Christianity claims God is a God of peace. If that is so, would it be possible for God to sanction war?

nine

The Just War

So, Christianity is pacifist, based on Jesus' teachings. This doesn't quite fit with such things as the Crusades and soldiers getting blessed by vicars and priests before they go to war. Somewhere along the line, Christians must have decided that it is fine to go to war.

Actually, quite early in Christian history, Christians decided they could fight. St Paul told early Christians to obey their leaders, who had been given their power by God. When their leaders ordered them to join the army (and fight), the dilemma was created. However, it is also true that Christians began to see reasons to justify war – war became seen as a necessary evil, and that made it tolerable. Look back to p81 and its list of wars. Which ones do you think Christians would see as justifiable?

In order to help Christians judge whether a war situation was just (and therefore fightable), criteria were put forward, firstly by St Augustine, then St Thomas Aquinas. Aquinas' set of guidelines hold true today – in fact, the US President, Bill Clinton, when announcing the start of the bombing of Serbia in 1998, went through them one by one to show his orders were just. The message is clear: sometimes, it is wrong to remain peaceful, because of the suffering and evil. Few Christians would disagree with the rightness of declaring war on Nazi Germany, in what became the Second World War, for example. Go back to p81. Could any of these be just wars?

▶ Is it possible to fight a war in the manner described in the guidelines? Think back to the early work you did about war and try to remember the problems you met there in terms of behaviour and management of war.

The Roman Catholic Church supports the Just War – 'While the danger of war remains … Governments cannot be denied the right to defence if they have exhausted every peaceful means of settlement.' *(Gaudum et Spes)*

Few Christians would support the idea of nuclear war, because it is not controllable. They may support the holding of nuclear weapons as a deterrent, but their use would be considered unjust.

The guidelines

① War must be started and controlled by a just leader.

② There is a just reason for the war, and those who are attacked deserve to be.

③ The war is carried out with the right intention – both aim and justification should be real and clear. The war continues only until that aim is achieved.

④ The war is fought in a just way – certain people are left alone, and certain standards of behaviour are observed by the soldiers.

The Basics

Investigating the Issue. Choose two religions from this unit. Use the information to answer these questions. Use concepts in other units to give additional support.

What do the words *war* and *peace* mean? Give an example of each t show you understand.

Why do wars happen? Do you think they are ever justifiable?

For each of the two religious traditions you have studied, explain the attitude to war, using quotations to back up your points.

In what circumstances might the traditions you have studied accept w

For all religions, peace is the ideal, even though the way to achieve i may be different. Explain the attitude of the two traditions to peace Use quotations to support your points.

War is an inevitable part of a world with humans in it. How far do you agree? Give reasons and explain the points you make showing you have considered more than one point of view.

► **The Muslim Attitude to War and Peace**

Peace

One meaning of the word *Islam* is peace.

> Allah (God) has 99 names known to man, these include <u>as salam</u> — the source of peace.

> Muslims should work to maintain peace — negotiation and mediation are better than war. They should always be the first and main option, not easily put aside.

> In the Qur'an it says 'Whenever those who believe in Our signs come to you, say Peace be upon you!' When two Muslims meet, they say this phrase in Arabic – <u>salaam alaikum</u>. They should not hold grudges against each other, and if they have had a quarrel, which is still unresolved after three days, the two Muslims should go to greet each other and lay the difference aside.

► If someone said to you that Islam is not a peaceful religion, how could you use these ideas to respond and demonstrate otherwise?

It is clear that Islam should be a religion of peace. It is said that if all people in the world were Muslim, and followed Islamic law, then there would only be peace. However, Islam does have another side, where war becomes a duty.

Jihad

This word means *struggle with one's utmost* – in other words fight as hard as you can. It actually refers to the fight that each person has within themselves to do the right thing, to behave correctly, to follow the rules laid down by Allah and live a pure life.

It also has another meaning – *holy war*. In the Qur'an, it is used when talking about waging war for defence against aggression, or fighting against a situation where attack by an enemy is inevitable. In disputes between nations then, negotiation must be the first option. However, if that fails, it becomes a duty to fight.

In the Muhammadan period of Islam, the Muslim community was forced to run away from Mecca, to save itself. After this event, because the Meccan people still wanted to kill them, Muslims were given an order by God to fight back when under attack. This is how holy war became a duty for Muslims. In the Qur'an it says, 'To these against whom war is made, permission is given to fight, because they are wronged' and 'Fighting is prescribed for you, and you dislike it … But Allah knows and you do not know.' Islam sees a need to help others, and to defend those being persecuted. To help maintain and establish peace, and to protect those who are persecuted are both Muslim ideals.

Trade wars turn nastier

Country invaded

All Muslims ordered out of the country

► Look at the headlines. Based on what you know, how should Muslims approach these situations? Which ones might Muslims be justified in declaring holy war for?

nine

Fighting a Holy War

There are strict rules in the Qur'an, and in Shariah about holy war. Much is similar to the rules of the Geneva Convention, of the Christian just war, and probably to the ones you thought of at the beginning of this Unit. Some are specifically because of the fear of the community being destroyed, a result of the early days.

Firstly, when should Muslims fight?

- Not all Muslims have to fight in a war, which is declared holy war. In the Hadith, Muhammad is reported to have requested one man in two to fight. This is common sense really, in a male-dominated society. Why?

- When on the battlefield, Muslims must fight – they must not run away. 'When you meet a force, be firm' *(Qur'an)*. Why?

- If a town is attacked, every person must fight. Why?

- When summoned to fight by a just and good ruler, Muslims should do so. If you are asked to join forces, you must fulfil your obligation. Why should such a ruler be respected like this?

Secondly, who should fight?

- Sane, Muslim men, who are old enough, and who can provide for their family until their return. So who should not and why?

Thirdly, how should a holy war be fought?

- A holy war only begins when the enemy has begun to fight 'Attack anyone who attacks you to the same extent as he attacked you' *(Qur'an)*. Similarly, when the enemy suggests peace, the Muslim should be peaceful. 'But if the enemies incline towards peace, you also incline towards peace, and trust in Allah!'

- Muslims must allow civilians to live their normal lives. They shouldn't attack or mistreat them, destroy their buildings, and especially not their places of worship. Their crops should be left alone. The first Caliph of Islam gave this and more as a code of conduct for soldiers.

- Prisoners of war should be well treated, for example, given enough food. Part of zakat can be used to feed captives – 'And they feed, for the love of Allah … the captive.' They must not be tortured or punished for being the enemy. They can be ransomed back to their own army.

▶ Why do you think Muslims are supposed to treat the enemy so well?

However, Muslims should do whatever they feel is necessary to deal with enemy prisoners and civilians if they cause problems. So, a resistance movement would be dealt with severely, for example. 'But if they have treacherous designs against you, they have already been in treason against Allah, and so He has given you power over them.' *(Qur'an)* They should still act in a just manner, however, as this is how Allah wants them to act.

The war ends when justice is restored, or when the enemy calls for peace.

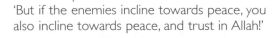

► The Buddhist Attitude to War and Peace

The spiritual leader of Tibetan Buddhism, the Dalai Lama. He won the Nobel Peace Prize in 1992.

How can we talk about Buddhism and war? It is almost impossible. The whole message of Buddhism is one of peace – peace within each of us, which affects how we deal with each other and the world. If we are peaceful, so is the world.

Buddhist countries do have armies or soldiers. They are often very small, and with quite limited training and resources. They are there for civil matters, and in the extreme circumstance of needing to protect the regent of the country. They are not there as an aggressive, outward looking force.

► *How can an army be used in these ways, and not be primarily a fighting force?*

Buddhism – a Faith Based on Compassion

All Buddhists follow the Five Precepts. These are guidelines on living as a Buddhist. They indicate the behaviour which is skilful and which will help in a person's quest for enlightenment or to live a good life. They also indicate unskilful behaviour. The first is to refrain from harming any sentient being. This act of non-harming is also called *ahimsa*. Naturally if we follow this precept, we will not even consider war. The act of harming is unskilful; its skilful equivalent is to show compassion and help others. Following the first precept cultivates that attitude, because we don't want to hurt those we respect. Since compassion and a desire for the well-being of others are key elements of Buddhist teaching, war must be excluded.

► *How will following this precept change a person's life in terms of what they do or don't do? How does it affect behaviour in conflict situations?*

Buddhists believe in reincarnation, that is, that all of our intentional acts, deeds and words will have a shaping influence on our future life or lifetimes. This can be negative or positive. Doing anything that is unskilful creates bad karma, and will have a negative effect on a

person's future. War involves killing – be it actual, or giving the order, or taking the decision to go to war. It must harm our rebirth.

► *How does this belief give a personal motivation for not harming others in war?*

Buddhists try to observe the Noble Eightfold Path in their lives. This is a set of eight practices which are methods of training the self. One of these is *Right Livelihood*, that is, having a job, which is not in conflict with Buddhist teaching. Trading in arms is specifically excluded from acceptable jobs.

► *Why might this be so? How is it tied to Buddhist teachings?*

During the Vietnam-US war one Buddhist monk killed himself and ensured photos were passed on to the world press to show his belief that the war was wrong.

One of the first Buddhist kingdoms was that led by the Emperor Asoka in Northern India in the third century BCE. He became a Buddhist after establishing his kingdom, and immediately enforced many rules, which are clearly Buddhist. He encouraged vegetarianism, banned animal sacrifice, and built positive relationships with the rulers of neighbouring countries, so that peace was possible. All of this was based on the first precept, and the compassion it brings.

► *Why should believing in non-violence lead to being compassionate?*

One image of the Buddha is that of Avalokiteshvara. This form is actually a Bodhisattva, that is, a being who has chosen not to attain Nirvana, because it feels so much compassion for other people and wants to help them. It has perfected *Bodhichitta* (genuine compassion). Avalokiteshvara is often seen with a thousand hands and a thousand eyes, to show he is looking to help everyone he can, and is able to do so. Anyone who asks is said to be helped.

This statue shows the Buddha in abhaya mudra position, a gesture of peace – his hands indicate the observer should not fear him.

The Bodhisattva of infinite compassion and mercy.

During the Vietnam–US war, monks were active in helping the victims of war. They did not fight, but did what they could to lessen the suffering of those affected. It is common for Buddhist monks to be involved in any work, which lessens suffering.

► *What sorts of jobs could Buddhists do in wartime, which would be skilful, and show their beliefs?*

A Man of Peace

The Dalai Lama is seen world-wide as a symbol of peace. He is the spiritual leader of the Tibetan people. He fled Tibet in 1959 after the Chinese had invaded, as it was felt he would be taken to Beijing away from his people. In exile, he leads the Tibetan Government. Thousands of Tibetans have left Tibet to be nearer to the Dalai Lama. In spite of regular demands for a more physical response to the Chinese, the Dalai Lama refuses to even consider violence. He believes that peace can only exist when the atmosphere is one of mutual respect, which comes from within ourselves. The key to creating a better and more peaceful world is the development of love and compassion for others. He has said that he is willing at any time to discuss peace for Tibet with the Chinese. In all of his speeches, he states and restates his position of a peaceful means as the only way to end conflict.

◄◄ Check out the details on Martin Luther King, another man of peace, in Unit 4, (p35).

Find out about the work of the Dalai Lama. How does he embody peace and compassion?

nine

Exam Tips

In previous years, the exam has asked you to consider a war in terms of the teachings of the religion you have studied. It is useful, then, for you to have an idea about a war of the 20th century.

The British Government declared war on Germany in 1939, after German troops had invaded Poland, with whom Britain had a treaty. The war ended in 1945, with surrender by Germany to allied troops. During the war, enemy troops who were captured were held in Prisoner-of-War camps, which were checked at intervals by representatives of the Red Cross. The British Government used bombing raids on Germany and German positions as part of its military campaign. These included the destruction of the city of Dresden – bombed almost out of existence.

▶ *Using the war in the account above, explain whether or not the two religion traditions you have studied would support or condemn participation by its followers.*

▶ *Go back to the beginning of the Unit (p81). In which situations would the two religious traditions you have studied possibly declare or join war?*

The application of concepts to issues has featured in past questions on this topic. Try these:

① Explain the terms *justice* and *sanctity of life*.
(2 marks)

② How might Christians apply each of these ideas to arguments about the morality of war? (8 marks)

What is wrong with the following attempts at answers? How can you change or improve the responses?

① Justice is fairness, getting things equal again. Like when one country invades another, and the first country fights back and gets rid of them. Then they get some sort of apology and compensation, so it's all fair. Sanctity of life is about how important or sacred life is. That means we shouldn't kill someone, because their life is too special for us to be able to do that. It is God's role, not ours.

② In war, you have to kill people, or order someone to kill others, or even decide to send your army to war in the first place. Everyone involved is linked to killing, so they all contribute to the idea that for some people life isn't special enough. It is okay to kill some people. If they believe in sanctity of life, maybe they won't want to be involved in killing – like the Quakers. Life is sacred, so it is wrong to kill.

Try these evaluative questions:

(a) *You have to work at peace to keep it.* How far do you agree? Give reasons and explain your answer.

(b) *Nuclear war can never be a just war.* How far do you agree? Give reasons and explain your answer.

In answer 1, there are only two marks available, and the question simply asks for an explanation. To just define each word or phrase is enough. The rest is nice to read, but in effect wasted time.

In answer 2, only half of the question is answered. Both justice and sanctity of life have to be discussed, not just one of them. This answer threw away four marks before the examiner had even read it.

10

The Natural World

hunting brings another species to extinction

the Amazon rainforest is shrinking

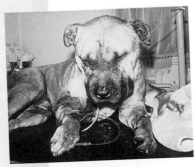

dog fighters imprisoned

Does the world belong to humans? Can we use it in whatever way we see fit?

The answers to these questions may well decide how we think of the natural world, and how we treat it. They are certainly the key to religious thinking.

> Go through the newspapers for the next two weeks. Keep a record of all the stories involving humans and nature. Look at the overall picture – how are we treating the natural world? Are we using it as we wish, or are we taking measures to protect it? What measures are being taken? Why should we do things to look after it?

This Unit is focused around several concepts. The first is one we have met already – sanctity of life. All of nature is life, so should the idea of life being sacred extend to the natural world? What about animals? If it does, the implications are massive.

Next, we have the concept of stewardship, or the role of looking after, in this case, the world and everything natural. If humans have this role, what can we say about how well we are dealing with it?

The Unit looks at specific ideas and you need to consider the following points:

- Does the world belong to us?
- Do we have a duty or role to take care of the world?
- Does all life, including animals and nature, deserve respect?
- How can we make a contribution to the environmental problems now existing?
- How can we show respect for other forms of life on earth?

Cats now the No1 household pet

research laboratory raided by animal rights campaigners

more medicine finds in rainforest

▶ Whose World Is It?

Newsflash — Local Government has today agreed to allow the new bypass around the town. It involves some 600 acres of greenbelt, previously protected, and some farming land. It will involve the destruction of the habitats of several endangered species. Relocation of the popular Great Green Children's Park, which will also be lost, will be considered at some point in the future. It will mean safer roads in town, because of rerouting the increasing amounts of heavy goods traffic. This will also have an impact on air pollution, which is currently a major problem and a recognised contributory factor to increased levels of bronchial complaints and asthma in our young and old. Parts of the old road will be converted to pedestrian zones, and some new housing will be constructed to ease housing shortages. The rebuilding will lead to the demolition of several very old streets, which have archaic sewerage systems. Plans to redevelop the disused factory complex have now been dropped to help fund the road scheme and its side effects.

Read the above. Make a list of the pros and cons of this scheme.

Use this list to construct arguments to support the scheme, and to protest against it; these arguments will be presented at a public meeting. Do this from the points of view of the following people:

① a mother with young children

② a local farm owner, who has fallen on difficult times

③ a local environmental specialist, whose specialism is endangered species

④ a local motorist (family man) who uses the route every day

⑥ the owner of a construction company who may be contracted to do some of the work

It isn't just a case of having to respect a duty of stewardship, or about us being superior to nature. There is a need to help humans, which must be balanced with caring for the environment. People have different vested interests, which will affect their view.

▶ Can there ever be a balance, which protects both human and environmental interests?

Muddying the Waters

The whole environmental issue is further complicated by other conflicting interests. There is an issue about how we treat the world, and whether we have the right to do as we wish. You could say that Genesis gives us the world. We can choose to do what we want with things that belong to us.

Improved technology has drastically increased the rate of our destruction of the earth.

▶ *Can you think of examples of how increased technological capability have led to greater environmental impact?*

We can't say the technological advances have been wrong. They have improved our lives so much – we now live longer, are healthier, and have better standards of living. However, that damage has future implications, and these have shocked some people into calling for greater awareness of environmental problems, and more action to solve them. What are the future implications?

A further issue is that of the poorer countries in the less economically developed world. As these countries try to improve standards for themselves, they move into greater use of technology and that damages their own environment. China, for example, pollutes on a massive scale, but justifies it in the quest for a better life for its people. Is it morally right for us to deny countries the chance to improve? We have already passed through a similar phase, but before environmental problems were understood. Is there a solution to this? Additionally, population increase creates a need for more land and so leads to natural environments being destroyed – greenbelt land in Britain is under threat by new housing, for example. People do need to live somewhere.

We have made use of animals in many ways throughout history – as food, friend, clothing, servant, sport. It isn't easy to just stop using animals overnight.

▶ *How do we make use of animals? Which ways do you find acceptable? Are some uses so important that the suffering they cause to animals is justified? Explain.*

There is a conflict between looking after the world, and improving life for people, or even giving a fair chance to all people. Religious traditions have to work this out.

► The Christian Attitude to the Natural World

In Genesis we are told that God created everything in the world, and that he saw it was good.

Matthew 5 v 26 — Look at the birds of the air: they neither sow nor reap nor gather into barns, and yet your heavenly Father feeds them.

Genesis 9 v 2–3 They (animals) are all placed under your power. Now you can eat them as well as green plants; I give them all to you for food.

Genesis 9 v 9–17 speaks of God making a covenant with every human and every living creature to never again destroy the earth. The rainbow is the sign of that covenant.

Genesis 1 v 26 Let us make man in our image . . . let them have dominion over . . . all the earth.

Psalms 24 v 1 The earth is the Lord's and everything in it.

What impression do these quotes give you about how Christians should view animals and the rest of the natural world? Try to remember some of them: by using them in answers, you can give a general response to a question about attitudes to the natural world.

Speaking as a Catholic

Since early in their history, Christians have spoken about the sanctity of all life on earth, because it is the work of God.

The current Pope, John Paul II, has spoken on many occasions about this subject. His teachings show that we should cherish the world God has given us, and should look after it as a duty. Stewardship can be seen as an act of worship – by doing God's work, we are showing our love for him.

St Basil – I want to awake in you a deep admiration for creation, until you in every place, contemplating plants and flowers, are overcome by a living remembrance of the Creator.

We cannot interfere in one area of the ecosystem without paying due attention both to the consequences of such interference in other areas and to the well-being of future generations.

Respect for life and the dignity of the human person also extends to the rest of creation, which is called to join man in praising God.

More than ever – individually and collectively – people are responsible for the future of the planet.

Pope John Paul II

Roman Catholic teaching suggests that we have been given the responsibility of caring for the earth by God. This involves looking after and protecting all of nature. If we link this to the idea of Judgement Day, which is part of Catholic belief, it is wise to carry out this duty. On Judgement Day we will be judged according to what we have done or not done. If we didn't do anything to try to protect nature, we may be punished.

It is necessary and urgent to abandon ill-considered forms of dominating custody of all creatures. I am happy to encourage and to bless all those who work so that animals may be considered and treated in a Franciscan way, as brothers and sisters.

Scientists must abandon laboratories and factories of death.

Pope John Paul II

These statements make clear the attitude of the Catholic Church to animals. They are special, their lives are sacred. Anyone whose work helps with the recognition of animals as God's creation, is regarded highly. They are doing God's work.

Franciscan refers to St Francis of Assisi, who gave up his wealth to be a monk. He spent his life trying to live in harmony with nature. He is widely respected as the Patron Saint of animals. His belief was that animals are part of creation, and as such deserve respect and protection, even worship.

We use animals in many ways – farming, experimentation, and hunting are just three. We keep some animals as pets, and call them our friends.

▶ Which ways that we use animals do you think the Pope would see as acceptable? Can you justify any?

Speaking as a Methodist

The Methodist Church has put together its own environmental policy, presented in June 2000. It sees the environment and animal rights as major issues for the Church to be involved in. In its statement it reaffirms that the Christian mission includes caring for God's earth.

The **Methodist** Church

This Christian mission is seen to have many elements:

Firstly, that Christians are privileged to be the stewards of God's earth, and are partners in creation with the natural world.	Secondly, that part of our duty as Christians is to sort out problems we have created between humans and nature, to create a new balance as God originally intended.	Thirdly, to adopt good practices which will help sustain the environment and not worsen it further. This must be done especially in the light of future generations.

► *How do you think Methodists could show each of these in their lives and actions? What could they do to meet these aims?*

The policy further said that the need to look after the world was an issue for all Christians, and so different denominations should work together on it. An inter-denominational group called the Christian Ecology Movement now exists.

► *Why should Christians want to work together on this issue?*

Focus on Experimentation

We use animals for experimentation. This may be to test:

*   the effectiveness of a new medicine (how effective it is, what are the side effects)

*   the toxicity of a new product (how much of it can be consumed before it kills or maims)

*   the excessive use or lack of use of something (e.g. how we are affected by not sleeping).

There are many groups opposed to the use of experimentation. They claim it is cruel (e.g. the Draize test functions through dripping liquid into a rabbit's eye to see the whole range of its effects) and unnecessary (we can now use tissue cultures from humans to do tests on) and also ineffective as we are different from animals and so tests can never be guaranteed.

The Basics

Choose two religious traditions from the preceding three or following four pages to answer these questions.

①
For the religious traditions you have chosen, outline the attitude of that tradition to the environment. Use quotations to support your outline.

②
How might that attitude be translated into actions? How might a relig believer carry out those ideas?

③
Outline the attitude of two traditions to animals.

④
Why might some religious believers agree with some uses of animals, but not others? Use examples to back up the points you make.

⑤
Animal experiments should be totally banned. Do you agree? Give reasons and explain your answer. Refer to religious teachings in your answer.

Focus on Hunting

Hunting came from a need to find food. Fur was recognised as a good material in the cold before synthetic materials were invented. It is today also a sport. Many people find hunting for food to be acceptable. It is usually caught and killed with minimum suffering to the animal. However, hunting for fur, or hunting for sport are considered unacceptable by many. When fur is for fashion, it leads to the farming of naturally wild animals which are unnaturally caged throughout their lives. Hunting for sport relies on a catch which takes the time, skill and guile of the hunter – a quick catch and kill is no challenge. Both then lead to immense suffering on the part of animals.

► The Buddhist Attitude to the Natural World

> Destruction of nature and natural resources results from ignorance, greed, and lack of respect for the earth's living things ... This lack of respect extends to future generations who will inherit a vastly degraded planet.
>
> The earth is not only the common heritage of all humankind but also the ultimate source of life.
>
> Conservation is not merely a question of morality, but a question of our own survival.
>
> Dalai Lama

In the box (left) are quotations from the Dalai Lama, who is the best known and most prolific Buddhist writer of our time. His message is that peace must be our goal. This peace is not just between peoples and countries, but also within ourselves, and between ourselves and nature (see p89).

One of the central beliefs of Buddhism is that our constantly changing self will be reincarnated many times. That means it will be born into many lifetimes. The quality and opportunities of each lifetime are the result of our thoughts, words and behaviour in past lives. In simple terms, if I am a good person, I should have a positive rebirth.

A second belief is that all life is special, and should be respected. One of the Five Moral Precepts of Buddhism is to not cause harm to other sentient beings (see p98).

► Why should this have a massive implication for how I live my life in respect to the environment? Think of it in terms of what my rebirth may be.

► Is the message of conservation much stronger in Buddhism than in any other faith?

Vegetarianism in Buddhism

Most Buddhists are vegetarians simply because of the Fifth Moral Precept. They do not want to harm any sentient being. The precepts have a positive and negative way of being stated. *Do not harm* is negative. Positively put, this precept will encourage generosity and kindness to all sentient beings.

► *Can you think of some examples of how this might be carried out by Buddhists in terms of food?*

Some Buddhists will eat meat. In fact, Buddhists in Tibet, and in some other very high altitude places, need to for their diet. Also, if a monk is offered meat as a gift, he should eat it because it has been given in goodwill.

Meat-eating can be seen as a waste of resources – the same amount of land used to produce crops as that used to rear animals can feed far more people. It can also be seen as promoting a cruel practice for many farming methods may seem unkind to the animals. For a Buddhist, it is an act of compassion to be vegetarian.

Focus on Farming

Research on farming techniques can be quite eye-opening. It is important to have farms to produce the quantities of meat and dairy products which people require for their diets. It would be ridiculous to simply go out hunting for food when you wanted it. Early on in the history of humans, people learnt the benefit of farming. However, many people feel that farming – because it is a business – ignores the rights of animals. Animals are treated as objects, with no feelings or needs beyond food and water. This has allowed farming practices that do not take into account the potential suffering of animals. For example, hens are raised in cages which are too small for them to move around in; pigs are tethered in stalls for all of their lives; calves are kept in cages in the dark to produce veal.

► *Is it right that animals should suffer just so that we can eat whatever we want to?*

Many people choose to be vegetarian because of what they see as unhygienic or cruel farming practices.

► The Jewish Attitude to the Natural World

A righteous man pays attention to the needs of his animal. *Proverbs 12 v 10*

(On the Sabbath day), you will not do any work … nor your animals. *Deuteronomy 5 v 14.*

The earth and everything that is in it is the Lord's. *Psalms 24 v 1*

Have dominion over the fish of the sea and over the birds of the air and over every living thing that moves upon the earth. *Genesis 1 v 28*

In Exodus, we are told that animals as well as humans are to be given a day of rest, fields are to be given a year of rest for every six years of usage, and three festivals are be to kept which thank God for the provisions of nature.

Genesis chapter one is the story of God's creation of the world. Everything God creates is seen as good, therefore it is special.

Judaism teaches that the world is God's creation and must be respected. All of nature, including humans, is a part of one amazing creation, and is an expression of God (because God just said 'let it be' and it was created).

treyfah – forbidden

► *What can you see in the quotations above which supports this idea?*

There is a duty not to destroy the world, as well as one to protect it, because we are borrowing the world from God – it belongs to God, not us.

Judaism sees that people have a higher position within nature than animals and therefore animals can be used.

► *How do the quotes above support this idea? In what ways might Jews see it as acceptable to use animals?*

Even though we can make use of animals for our needs, we still have to respect them, and should not abuse the position God has given us.

Jewish Food Laws

Perhaps these give us a better insight into using animals, but treating them kindly. These laws are found in Leviticus chapter 11 and Deuteronomy chapter 14. They list the types of animals, often naming specific ones, which Jews may or may not eat. The animals which may be eaten must have been killed in a specific way. This is called *shechitah* killing, and it takes five years to be trained as a Jewish butcher (schochet). Once in business, a schochet will be inspected regularly to ensure his establishment and methods remain kosher (i.e. acceptable to Jewish law). When animals are killed, they should not suffer – the whole process from taking to slaughter to the slaughter itself is designed to minimise this. Before slaughter a prayer is said to thank God for the animal.

treyfah – forbidden

► *In what ways might an animal suffer when about to be slaughtered? Does your answer reveal anything about how you think about animals?*

Exam Tips

Remember – this topic will be covered by a 20 mark question. It is presented in the form of a structured essay, that is, several linked questions, each usually worth four or more marks. You have to be able to explain yourself, and give examples – in other words, breadth and depth are vital. You need to be able to remember and use religious teachings. You also have to be able to argue from more than one viewpoint.

▶ *What were the major concepts in this Unit?*

Stewardship and sanctity of life. These also have linked concepts – responsibility and creation. Put together, you get the idea that God created the world, over which he gave us the responsibility of stewardship, which means protecting and caring for all forms of life because of the sanctity of all life. You have to be able to recognise and define or explain these concepts. Can you?

1 Explain the terms *sanctity of life* and *stewardship*.

2 Explain the terms *creation* and *responsibility*.

3 How do each of the four concepts given above relate to the issue of the natural world? Give examples to illustrate your explanations.

In simply secular terms, you might be asked about problems. How much do you know?

4 State two ways in which the environment is being damaged.

5 Animals can be badly treated. Explain three examples of this.

6 Why might someone choose to be vegetarian?

7 How might someone show their disapproval of the way in which animals are treated?

You will certainly be asked about the attitude(s) of at least one religious tradition to the issue(s). Do you know them? Can you back them up with references to scripture/quotations?

8 Outline the teaching of one religious tradition you have studied on the issue of the environment.

9 Outline the teaching of one religious tradition you have studied on animal rights.

Finally, you will have to answer an evaluative question on this topic. These often bring up the conflict between what humans need and the sanctity of the environment and life. Try some.

10 *Religious believers should be more concerned about other people than about the environment.* Do you agree? Give reasons for your answer, showing that you have thought about more than one point of view.

11 *Life is sacred, but there is a pecking order which gives humans the power to use other lifeforms as they see fit.* Do you agree? Give reasons for your answer, showing that you have thought about more than one point of view.

How did you do?

Did you find those questions straightforward? Are you confident in your ability to cope? The questions you have seen cover the whole issue. Sometimes, though, they can seem very difficult because the question isn't directly from what you have learned. Look at the following. Can you answer them?

1 Outline the teachings of one religious tradition you have studied on the issue of vegetarianism.

2 How might Christians apply the concepts of *sanctity of life* and *stewardship* to arguments about the right and wrong use of natural resources?

3 *It's no good trying to save the rainforests if this means putting thousands of people out of work.* Do you agree? Give reasons for your answer, showing you have thought about more than one point of view.

Did you even know where to start? Let's look at them again.

Question one – easy if you have studied Buddhism. What if you didn't? You can still do a good job – use what you know. Choose the tradition. What does that tradition say about animals? Special creation? What does it say about life? Sacred? Is that all life? Have we been given stewardship or total power? If stewardship, that means looking after, so can we eat meat? If we can eat meat, we still have an obligation to look after, which means minimise suffering. So how can we do that? Are there any meat-eating practices, which might seem cruel, therefore not allowed? As long as you keep relating the teaching back to its specific relevance to vegetarianism, you're fine.

Question two – you may have been asked to define each in the previous question, so don't repeat yourself. How can we meet each concept in practice? Give examples to show each – both keeping and breaking. For example, life is sacred, including the environment. If we destroy habitats for road-building projects, then we destroy both animals and plant life – so it is wrong. A project, which moved such habitats, or catered for them and protected them (e.g. tunnels under roads for frogs and hedgehogs) meets the concept.

Question three – many levels on which to discuss this, so it is easy to cover the several views. Firstly, how important are the rainforests to human survival? (Lungs of the planet?) Secondly, who will be out of work – is there a global impact? (US burger joints may be stocked from cattle ranches on former rainforest land.) Thirdly, does deforestation have a direct human impact? (Forest tribes, and small-scale farmers left homeless.) Fourthly, does it have a wider impact to save the forests? (New medicines being found in the rainforest.) There are lots of ideas to pick up and follow.

Appendix I

Revision Outline

The following is a revision guide. Generally it follows the outline of topics presented in this book. If you know all of the answers already when you read through it, you will probably do brilliantly. Use it as a checklist of what you know, and what you have yet to get to grips with. It could even serve as a last-minute check before you go into the exam. Each word should be recognisable to you. Each phrase should trigger a whole lot of ideas in your head – linked people, examples, explanations. When it does, you are ready.

UNIT	WORDS TO LEARN	TOPICS WITHIN UNIT
The Existence of God	Atheist Agnostic (Mono)theist Polytheist Creation Design Evolution	• Why people suggest God does exist • Why people suggest God doesn't exist • The Big Bang Theory • The argument from First Cause • A creation story • The Argument from Design • Evolution • People's experience of God • Reality and illusion
The Problems of Evil and Suffering	Evil Suffering Free Will Omnipotence Omniscience Benevolence	• The overall problem – why does a loving, powerful, knowing God allow evil and suffering? • The problem broken up – problems to do with God's love, God's power, God's creation … • Solutions to the problem – pain as education, punishment, test, free will defence, balance, the devil
The Nature of God	Immanent Transcendent Personal Impersonal Atheist Agnostic (Mono)theist Polytheist	• Description of God in two religious traditions • How and why people's knowledge of God differs • Why people prefer God to be …
General and Special Revelation	Revelation Special Revelation General Revelation	• Two examples of special revelation • The impact of special revelation • How we can know God through … nature • … worship – charismatic, contemplative, sacramental • … holy books and teachings • … the lives and work of people • The impact of general revelation • Reality or illusion – can we trust revelation?

UNIT	WORDS TO LEARN	TOPICS WITHIN UNIT
Ways of Making Moral Decisions	Absolute morality Relative morality	• How do we make decisions? What influences people generally? • What influences religious people? – holy books, teachings, leaders, God – examples of each • What place have reason, tradition or conscience – are they from God? • How is our behaviour affected by our beliefs and values?
Abortion	Abortion Sanctity of life Quality of life	• Why women have abortions • The law regarding abortion • The attitude of two traditions to abortion • Quotes to support the attitudes presented • Real examples of abortion, and the application of religious teachings to them
Sex, Marriage and Divorce	Celibacy Contraception Adultery Divorce Arranged marriage Commitment Responsibility	• Attitudes of two traditions to sex before marriage, and sex generally • Quotes to support the attitudes presented • Attitudes of two traditions to the use of contraception • Quotes to support the attitudes presented • Roles and responsibilities within marriage • Attitudes of two traditions to mixed faith marriage and mixed race marriage. • Attitudes of two traditions to divorce • How two traditions might try to help those with marital problems
Prejudice and Discrimination	Prejudice Discrimination Equality Justice Community Sexism Racism Homophobia	• Why people are prejudiced • How people act out their prejudices • The attitude of two traditions to prejudice generally • Application of that attitude to two specific types of prejudice • How religious traditions work against prejudice
World Poverty	Poverty Wealth Stewardship Community Justice Compassion Equality	• Why religious traditions help others • How religious traditions help others • The attitudes of two traditions to helping those less fortunate than themselves • The work of at least one religious organisation

War and Peace	War Peace Justice Sanctity of life Pacifism	• Why religious believers are often pacifists • Why religious believers will go to war • Explanation of *Just War* and its criteria • Explanation of *Holy War* and its criteria • The attitudes of two traditions to the concept of peace • Knowledge of at least one war to compare with Just and Holy wars.
The Natural World	Responsibility Stewardship Creation Sanctity of life Environment Vegetarianism	• The conflict between protecting the environment and meeting human needs • How people can help the environment • The attitudes of two traditions to the environment • The attitudes of two traditions to animals • The attitudes of two traditions to meat-eating • Application of those attitudes to the world around us and its upkeep

Appendix II

Sample Paper

> *The only part of this page you complete*

Surname		Other Names		
Centre Number		Candidate Number		
Candidate Signature				

Leave blank

General Certificate of Secondary Education
Summer 2003

RELIGIOUS STUDIES (SPECIFICATION B)   **3062/71**
Paper 1 Thinking about God and Morality

ASSESSMENT and
QUALIFICATIONS
ALLIANCE

Dateline

Time allowed: 1 hour 45 minutes

For Examiner's Use	
Question	Mark
1	
2	
3	
4	
5	
6	
Q W C	
TOTAL	
Examiner's Initials	

Instructions
- Use blue or black ink or ball-point pen.
- Fill in the boxes at the top of this page.
- You must answer **Question 1**.
- You must answer **Question 2**.
- You should answer **either Question 3 or Question 4**.
- You should answer **either Question 5 or Question 6**.
- Write your answers to Question 1 in the spaces provided in this booklet.
- Write your answers to all other Questions on the continuation sheets at the end of this booklet.
- If you use any additional sheets, tie them loosely to the back of this booklet.
- Do all rough work in this book or on the continuation sheets.
  Cross through any work you do not want marked.

Information
- The maximum mark for this paper is 83.
- Mark allocations are shown in brackets.
- You will be awarded up to 3 marks for quality of written communication.
  You are required to:
  - present relevant information in a form that suits its purposes;
  - ensure that text is legible and that spelling, punctuation and grammar are accurate, so that meaning is clear;
  - use a suitable structure and style of writing.

Advice
- You are advised not to spend more than 25 minutes on each Question.

> *Quality of Written Communication worth 3 marks at the most*

> *Important to read all of this – it tells you what to do and what not to do*

> Topic of question

> How many marks total per question

PART A

Answer **Question 1** in the spaces provided.

A 1   The Nature and Existence of God

Total for this question: *20 marks*

Read the following statements and then answer the questions below.

| Statement A: | God is the Creator |

| Statement B: | God is my conscience |

| Statement C: | God is a special kind of person |

| Statement D: | God does not exist |

| Statement E: | God is not a single Being but a unity of Beings |

> What each question is worth. Measure the size of your answer to the marks available

(a)   Which Statement would be made by an atheist?

Statement ....

(1 mark)

(b)   Explain what Statement A means.

....

....

....

(2 marks)

(c)   Why would many religious believers disagree with Statement B?

....

....

....

....

....

....

....

....

(4 marks)

Words in italics are trigger words – vital to the question

(d)   What problems might there be in thinking of God as a *person* (Statement C)?

....

....

....

....

....

....

....

....

(4 marks)

(e)   Give one detailed argument against Statement D.

....

....

....

....

....

(4 marks)

(e)   Would religious believers agree with Statement E?

Give reasons for your answer, showing that you have thought about more than one point of view.

....

....

....

....

....

....

....

Need to answer from two sides

(5 marks)

These are all 'structured essays' which means that all of the parts of the question are linked

You must do QB2 – it is compulsory

These are the sheets of lined paper at the back of the book

PART B

You may remove pages 5 to 7 if you wish.

Answer **Question 2** on the continuation sheets.

Answer **either Question 3 or Question 4** on the continuation sheets.

Answer **either Question 6 or Question 7** on the continuation sheets.

Don't do both. If you do, both will be marked and you will get the mark for the question best answered. However, you have wasted a lot of time, and this leaves less for the other questions. Inevitably you get fewer marks

B 2   Evil and suffering   **Total for this question:** *20 marks*

(a)   What problems are raised for religious believers by evil and suffering?

(9 marks)

(b)   Explain how believing in God can help people to cope with suffering in their lives.

(6 marks)

(c)   "Without suffering and evil in the world, people would not turn to God or become better people."

Do you agree? Give reasons for your answer, showing that you have thought about more than one point of view. Refer to religious teachings in your answer.

(5 marks)

ANSWER EITHER QUESTION 3 OR QUESTION 4

B 3   Abortion   **Total for this question:** *20 marks*

A pregnant women has been told that she will have a severely handicapped child.

(a)   (i)   Explain why believers in **one** religious tradition are against abortion in the situation above.

(5 marks)

(ii)   Explain why believers in a **different** religious tradition think that abortion may be justified in the situation above.

(4 marks)

(b)   State and explain **two** circumstances, **other than the example above**, when abortion is regarded by some religious believers as acceptable.

(6 marks)

(c)   "If a baby is not wanted by its mother, there are many people who would adopt it. It should not be killed."

Do you agree? Give reasons for your answer, showing that you have thought about more than one point of view. Refer to religious teachings in your answer.

(5 marks)

OR

B 4 Prejudice and Discrimination   **Total for this question:** *20 marks*

(a)   Choose **two** different religious traditions and outline the teachings of each about prejudice and discrimination.

(9 marks)

(b)   How do people in **one** religious tradition apply their beliefs about prejudice and discrimination in practical ways?

(6 marks)

(c)   "By sending their children to religious schools, some religious believers are encouraging their children to be prejudiced against others."

Do you agree? Give reasons for your answer, showing that you have thought about more than one point of view.

(5 marks)

Again a choice. One or the other, not both

ANSWER EITHER QUESTION 5 OR QUESTION 6

B 5 War and Peace   **Total for this question:** *20 marks*

(a)   Choose **one** religious tradition.
Outline teachings which might help a religious believer to decide whether fighting a war is right or wrong.
You may use teachings from sacred texts and statements made by the authorities of this tradition in your answer.

(4 marks)

(b)   (i)   Explain the terms 'justice' and 'sanctity of life'.

(2 marks)

(ii)   How might Christians apply **each** of these ideas to arguments about the morality of war?

(9 marks)

(c)   "If there were no religions, there would be no wars."

Do you agree? Give reasons for your answer, showing that you have thought about more than one point of view. Refer to religious teachings in your answer.

(5 marks)

OR

B 6   The Natural World   **Total for this question:** *20 marks*

(a)   Choose **one** religious tradition.
         Outline teachings which might help a religious believer to decide how to use the Earth's resources.
         You may use teachings from sacred texts and statements made by the authorities of this tradition in your answer.

(4 marks)

(b)   (i)   Explain the terms 'sanctity of life' and 'stewardship'.

(2 marks)

         (ii)   How might Christians apply **each** of these ideas to arguments about the right and wrong use of natural resources?

(9 marks)

(c)   "It's no good trying to save the rainforests if this means putting thousands of people out of work."

         Do you agree? Give reasons for your answer, showing that you have thought about more than one point of view. Refer to religious teachings in your answer.

(5 marks)

There is a total of 20 marks available on the paper for this type of question – so make sure you practise them and can do them

END OF QUESTIONS

Glossary

agnostic a person who believes there are reasons for God's existence, and against it. Hence, remain unsure or open-minded

Allah the name of God in Islam, meaning 'One God'

Anthropic Principle evaluation of scientific evidence in relation to the universe; can be read in two ways, one to prove God, the other to ignore God

Apostles Creed a statement of Christian belief – from the Latin Credo, meaning 'I believe …'

atheist a person who believes God does not exist

avatar a divine consciousness born as a human, who is aware of their specialness and their role – Hindu faith

BCE Before Common Era

belief what someone accepts as being true for them

benevolent all-loving, loves each of us as individuals

Bible holy book of Christianity

Big Bang Theory scientific theory about the origins of the universe

Brahman ultimate reality in Hindu belief; God

CE Common Era

Charles Darwin 1809–1862; author of *Origin of the Species* (1859), which discussed ideas of evolution

creation general religious explanations of how the universe came about

Dalai Lama the political and spiritual leader of Tibet and Tibetan Buddhism

design a preliminary plan or idea for something to be established

devil/Satan the supreme spirit of evil

empirical evidence evidence verified scientifically

evolution theory of development of life from simple to complex forms

First Cause argument to prove the existence of God, based on God as First Cause of the world

fundamentalist a person who believes that the Bible is dictated by God and contains no errors

general revelation indirect experience of God, for example, the Bible contains the word of God but must be interpreted by people

Genesis first book of the Bible; refers here to the creation story shared by Christians and Jews

Gospel writers the four people who wrote the accounts of the life of Jesus – Matthew, Mark, Luke and John

Guru Granth Sahib holy book of Sikhism; collected poems and songs written by Gurus, mainly about God

Hindu creation myth the Hindu story for the beginning of the world

illusion a false belief; a something wrongly believed to exist; deceptive appearances

immanent God is involved in his creation e.g. in the person of Christ in the world

impersonal meaning that people cannot relate to God personally

infallible incapable of being wrong

malevolent wanting others to suffer, to want to cause ill to others

miracle an event which is contradictory to the normal order of things – usually applied to an action of God

mitzvot the 613 laws from the Torah that Jews must follow

monotheist a person who believes One God exists

moral evil the pain caused by the words and actions of humans

morality the sense of right and wrong

Muhammad ﷺ the last and final prophet of God in Islam

myth a widely held idea presented in story form

natural suffering pain caused by the activities of nature

omnipotent all-powerful; as powerful as it is possible to be: includes the ability to create the world

omniscient all-knowing, knows everything it is possible to know

Origin of the Species book written by Charles Darwin (1859) regarding evolution

paradise a state of complete bliss often used as a reference to God's Garden of Eden

personal relating to God described in human terms – he listens, speaks, cares, knows etc

polytheist a person who believes that many gods exist

proof a fact or thing that helps to show the truth

Qur'an the name of the Muslim Holy Book

reality what is real or actually exists

religious experience an experience which leaves one feeling one has met God in some way

revelation when God reveals himself to humans

Saul in the New Testament, he was a Jew who became a Christian known as Paul

shariah Islamic law

special revelation direct revelation of God, e.g. meeting God

St Thomas Aquinas monk and theologian; wrote the First Cause argument

Surah the word for 'chapter' in the Qur'an

teleological argument argument to prove God's existence through evidence of design in the world

theist a person who believes that One God exists

Torah holy book of Judaism; first five books of the Bible

transcendent in relation to God, beyond space and time – limitless

Trimurti Hindu godhead of Brahma, Vishnu and Shiva

Trinity Christian idea of the three parts of God– Father, Son and Holy Spirit

undeserved something that happens to a person which is not just or right

William Paley 1743–1805; put forward a teleological argument for the existence of God

Index